W9-BZU-292

In the Beginning . . .

THERE WERE NO DIAPERS

In the Beginning...

THERE WERE NO DIAPERS

Laughing and Learning
in the First Years of Fatherhood

Tim Bete

Sorin Books Notre Dame, Indiana

---

www.sorinbooks.com

International Standard Book Number: 1-893732-87-8

Cover and text design by David R. Scholtes

Printed and bound in the United States of America.

Library of Congress Cataloging-in-Publication Data
Bete, Timothy P.
  In the beginning-- there were no diapers : laughing and
learning in the first years of fatherhood / Timothy P. Bete.
      p. cm.
  ISBN 1-893732-87-8 (pbk.)
  1. Fathers--Humor. 2. Fatherhood--Humor. I. Title.

PN6231.F37B48 2005
814'.6--dc22

                                        2004020865

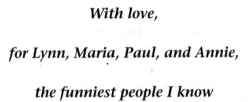

With love,

for Lynn, Maria, Paul, and Annie,

the funniest people I know

Contents

Acknowledgments 8

1 Botta Bing, Botta Boom—The Sound of Miracles 9

2 How I Determined the
   Sex of Our Baby—The Miracle of Birth 15

3 The Miraculous World of Potty Training........... 26

4 Dad's Service Center, and Other
   Miracles of the Night.. 36

5 It's a Miracle My Wife and I Are Sane
   (We Are, Aren't We?) 45

6 Ten Commandments Plus 672 Rules—
   If My Kids Obeyed It'd Be a Miracle 55

7 The Parable of the Dirty Laundry,
   and Other Miraculous Lessons........................... 65

8 The Miracle of Parent-Child Communication..... 74

9 Five Loaves, Two Fish—What, No Tartar Sauce?
   (or, My Son Ate a Vegetable—It's a Miracle!) ...82

10 Daddy's NOT Going to Buy You a Mockingbird,
   and Other Miraculous Ways to Save Money....... 93

11 My Wife Has Miraculous Superpowers 103

12 In the Beginning There Was No Duct Tape,
   and Other Miraculous Do-It-Yourself Projects.. 113

13 A Perfect Child—The Miracle of Christmas 122

14 Where's Moses When You Need Him?
   Miracles to Rid Your House of Plagues............ **133**

15 Finding First Base—The Miracle of Sports........ **141**

16 Miracles in the Air... **153**

17 God's Big Aquarium and the Miracle of Easter 162

18 I Am a Modern Miracle...................................... **170**

19 A Miracle-Filled Future..................................... **180**

Acknowledgments

In 1948, Erma Bombeck quietly slipped a humorous essay under the office door of Brother Tom Price, SM, a University of Dayton English professor.

"He said to me three magic words: 'You can write,'" Erma recalled. "It's all I needed as an impetus to keep going, and it sustained me for a very long time."

Special thanks to Teri Rizvi at the University of Dayton for acting as my Brother Tom Price and inviting me to work on the Erma Bombeck Writers' Workshop. Every writer deserves to be blessed with a mentor such as Teri.

Thanks to the thousands of readers who subscribe to my column and encouraged me to write this book. Your kind e-mails have meant more to me than you can imagine.

Thanks to all the editors who have published my column in the past. In a special way I'd like to thank Tom Allen at CatholicExchange.com, Owen Thomas at *The Christian Science Monitor*, and Ryan Warner, who gave me my first experience on radio. Thanks to Debra Hampton who was the first editor to believe I could write a book and Dan Driscoll for his friendship and masterful editing.

This book wouldn't have been possible without the inspiration from family. My parents were the first to show me God's love through laughter. Shortly after, my siblings taught me that making our parents laugh was the best way to get out of trouble. My wife Lynn and children, Maria, Paul, and Annie, provide some of the best dialogue a writer could want. They are truly the funniest people I know.

Finally, to God goes all the glory. (Note to publisher: God said it was okay for the royalty checks to go to me.)

Botta Bing, Botta Boom— The Sound of Miracles

When our daughter Anna Maria was born, she slept a lot—except when we wanted her to sleep. She would sleep in my arms. She would sleep in a car seat. But if we put her in her bassinet, her eyes popped open wide as if she had just seen a gallon of milk or a shiny new pacifier. I should have remembered from my high school French class that the literal translation of *bassinet* is "sleepless parent." *Je suis un bassinet.*

My first night of sleeplessness wasn't too difficult. But after a week I was delirious, and I don't mean in the happy sense. I considered signing up as a subject in a sleep deprivation experiment just to get some rest.

I kept a journal during our first week with Annie at home.

Day 1—Yawning: Only two hours of sleep but I'm so happy about the new addition to our family that it hasn't fazed me. Drank two cups of coffee to take the edge off my sleepiness. Watched three infomercials at 2 a.m. while rocking Annie to sleep. Resisted the temptation to buy a

Chia Pet in the shape of Jay Leno's head. Decided I would try to take a nap tomorrow.

Day 2—Groggy: The daytime nap didn't materialize. Used twice as much coffee in the coffee maker and cut the amount of water in half. Drank four cups. Starting to feel a little disoriented from lack of sleep. Our other children have noticed I'm a little grumpier than usual.

Day 3—Dazed: No sleep again. Can't make the coffee fast enough. Filled our water softener with coffee grounds instead of salt. Now we have java coming out of every fixture in the house. Beginning to hallucinate from lack of sleep. Had a great conversation with the toaster oven. Seems she has a crush on our George Foreman Grill.

Decided I should get some other chores done since I'm awake—although not coherent. Watered all the plastic plants in the house. Sent our dishes outside and put the cat in the dishwasher. Didn't realize we had a cat.

Day 4—Zombie-like: Annie was up again all night. Called the water softener company to see if they had a unit that makes espresso. Fell asleep for about an hour. Dreamt I was sailing to the new world with Christopher Columbus. Three ships were making the trip: the Niña, the Pinta, and the Anna Maria. The Anna Maria's sails were huge diapers. I was in charge of swabbing the poop deck. Awoke to the sound of Annie's cry. I was still in charge of swabbing the poop deck. Called the water softener company and told them I'd pay for rush delivery. Received a call from our neighbor asking if I had seen his cat.

Day 5—Comatose: No sleep again. Can't stay awake a minute longer. Resorted to putting a fistful of coffee grinds between my cheek and gum. Mmmmmm. Genuine coffee pleasure without the annoyance of holding a mug. My eyes are as red as radishes and I haven't shaved since Annie was born. When I answered the doorbell today, the two Girl Scouts selling cookies dropped their wares and ran in terror.

Received a phone call from the president of a major coffee company who said I was chosen as customer of the year and would receive a lifetime supply of coffee. Told him that I had already consumed a lifetime supply of coffee in the past five days.

Took an "Are You Sleep Deprived?" quiz I found in a supermarket tabloid.

1. Do you need an alarm clock in order to wake up at the appropriate time?

No. To wake up, I'd have to first be asleep.

2. Do you have trouble remembering?

Yes. Especially my name and where I live.

3. Do you often fall asleep while doing other activities?

ZZZzzzzzzzzz....

Then one night—botta bing, botta boom—Annie slept for eight straight hours. It seemed like a miracle. Our prayers had been answered.

"Botta bing, botta boom" is a term people use when they really mean, "I have no idea what happened, but I suspect a higher power was involved." For example, while the creation of the world took six days to complete, it can be summarized in just fourteen words: In the beginning was God, then—botta bing, botta boom—there was everything else. This is known as the Botta Bing, Botta Boom Theory of Creation—not to be confused with the Big Bang Theory, which was much louder and would have awoken the neighbors if they had already been created.

Some "botta bing, botta boom" moments are more spectacular than others. Being a parent changes your perspective about what constitutes a miracle. Before my wife and I had kids, I rarely thought about miracles. Now that we have three children—Maria (age seven), Paul (age five), and Annie (age two)—I experience miracles all the time, even if they are what some people would consider the minor variety.

If I had to list the top three miracles of all time, they would be the creation of the world, the parting of the Red Sea, and my son's potty training. You might question whether my son's learning to use the john is really in the same category with the creation of the world. I'll admit, I pondered that question for quite a while too. Then I realized the key difference: God didn't have to bribe the world into existence using M&Ms or sit next to Adam for hours reading *The Little Engine That Could* to coax Eve into popping out of Adam's rib.

When our son was two, and my wife and I had cleaned pee off the kitchen floor for the tenth time because he wasn't able to make it to the bathroom, potty training began to appear as miraculous and unlikely as the parting of the Red Sea. And, when the wonderful day arrived and he put on his first pair of "big boy" underwear, we thanked God as if we had just escaped from bondage, which in a sense we had. Our bondage just came in the form of size-five Pampers instead of Pharaoh. Potty training may be a minor miracle, but it's still a miracle if you have eyes to see it.

When I was in kindergarten, I prayed for proof that God existed. I wasn't looking for God to reveal himself through the biggest miracle. I was only five, so I was practical. I wanted God to place some graham crackers in a plastic bag in my coat pocket. Every day when I went into the coatroom, I dug my hands down deep into my pockets—but they were always empty. When I graduated to first grade, I gave up asking God for graham crackers because I was convinced he wasn't going to produce.

Thirty-five years passed. Then one day, I put my hand in my pocket and felt a plastic bag. I pulled it out, and there in the bottom of the bag were three graham crackers. Sure, they belonged to one of my kids, but who's to say God didn't just take the slow fulfillment route—using my daughter as the delivery girl—to grant my kindergarten prayer?

But that wasn't all. As I dug my hand deeper into my coat pocket, I discovered two rubber bands, a dandelion, some pebbles, and a Happy Meal prize. When God answers prayers, he does it in abundance. I showed these treasures to a friend, who showed me the contents of his pocket— two licorice sticks, three pennies, and a feather. I didn't have to ask him what he prayed for in kindergarten.

Minor miracles aren't as glamorous as their larger counterparts, but they have a powerful impact on life. It's no small event when your daughter rides her bike without training wheels for the first time or your new baby sleeps through the entire night. God uses minor miracles the way we use M&Ms for potty training. He coaxes us along through life with them. Minor miracles are God's way of reading *The Little Engine That Could* to us.

And, now that my eyes have been opened to minor miracles, they arrive on a daily basis.

How I Determined the Sex of Our Baby—
The Miracle of Birth

Having a baby is one of the greatest miracles a person can experience. And like most major miracles, there are a lot of minor miracles that tag along for the ride.

When baby Jesus was born, there were the miracles of the star, the angels appearing to the shepherds, and the wise men bearing gifts. When our children were born, I didn't see any stars, angels, gold, frankincense, or myrrh. But, the fertility police helped me remember a little trick I originally learned in my high school biology class—how to determine the sex of a baby before the child is born.

Every time my wife is pregnant, the fertility police immediately begin their stakeout. They were especially active when my wife was pregnant with our third child. If we didn't already have a boy and a girl, the fertility police may have left us alone. But with one child of each flavor, the members of the family-planning inquisition were chomping at the bit.

The fertility police look like mild-mannered shoppers but are actually a plainclothes procreation posse made up of census-taker wannabes who are willing to grill you with personal questions in any public setting. They must know if a woman is pregnant, how many children she has, and how many more she plans to conceive.

"Do you know if you're having a boy or a girl?" asked the woman behind us in the supermarket checkout line.

"Yes," I replied with confidence. Then I waited. After about a minute of silence she inquired indignantly, "Well, which is it—a boy or a girl?"

I told her I hadn't decided yet. This left her perplexed until I launched into my high school biology lecture.

"The male of the species determines the sex of the offspring," I began in my best academic drone. "I am the male, therefore, I decide the sex of our child. I will make my decision sometime between now and when the baby is born." (I skipped a few biology classes but think I got the gist of it.)

"Until our baby is born I can change my mind as many times as my little heart desires," I concluded. The woman pulled back her cart and changed checkout lanes, eyeing me suspiciously all the while.

Sometimes, the fertility police are in a playful mood and will venture a guess about the sex of your baby. "It's a boy, isn't it?" they ask.

"Nope," I reply.

"Ah! It's a girl," they conclude triumphantly.

"No, not a girl," I respond. (Because I alone determine the sex of our child, I routinely switch from girl to boy between questions.)

When accused of not knowing what my child is, I simply flash an all-knowing smile and say, "I'm the *only* one who knows if our baby is a boy or a girl." I get a lot of dirty looks in the checkout line.

The fertility police don't limit their questioning to the unborn. They also probe the size of your family and how your new child will fit in.

"I see you have a boy and a girl," they say, mastering the obvious. "Why are you having another child?"

"We can't figure out where these things keep coming from," I respond. "Do you have any idea?" It's surprising how easily some people blush.

Our friends who have four or more kids really get the treatment. When they parade through the grocery store, they're assaulted with, "Are all those yours?!" The question is asked as if the parents were holding an armful of nuclear bombs about to detonate.

Claiming you had four children on purpose will ensure a lecture on the pitfalls of large families. There is, however, one response that will silence the detectives.

Look protectively at your children and say, "Yes, all these are mine. I found them on sale in aisle five—buy three, get the fourth free." Then, follow up with, "Hey, the sign says, 'ten items or less.' I only have four kids, three bags of chips and a two-liter bottle of soda, so I'm under the limit."

What do the fertility police do with this information? They spread the word to other fertility officers in the vicinity. "Look at that woman over there," they gossip. "She has two kids and is having another one!"

"But stay away from her husband," they warn. "He's a nut case."

Even more miraculous than avoiding the fertility police is the math involved in becoming a parent. I know how to add. But, how can it be that no matter how carefully you plan your time, there is always one more task to complete before your baby's due date? This is especially true for first-time parents, who have a thinking disturbance that causes them to imagine they can remodel their entire home before their baby is born, even though the wife has been having contractions—forty-five seconds apart—for two hours. My wife and I had this disorder, which I call stop-the-clock-itis.

Stop-the-clock-itis usually starts with a simple task, such as painting the baby's room. Before you can blink it's evolved into painting an exact reproduction of Michelangelo's Sistine Chapel on the ceiling of the baby's room. But, first, you'll need to add an addition to your home as well as take four years of painting lessons. The thinking disorder prevents expectant parents from realizing it will be difficult to take four years of painting lessons in nine months. Those with advanced stages of stop-the-clock-itis convince themselves they can paint the ceiling in the two hours between going to church and visiting the in-laws for dinner.

When my wife was overdue with our third child, the doctor gave her a "non-stress test" in which a belt was put around her abdomen to measure the baby's movement. It is called a "non-stress" test because, compared to staying at home with a house full of kids, lying on a table with a belt around your tummy is relatively stress-free. It's the stress from multiple children that is the cure for pregnancy-induced stop-the-clock-itis. Just the right amount of stress and—botta bing, botta boom—your expectations are lowered. If you have more than five kids, your expectations will disappear entirely.

Stop-the-clock-itis has some long-term side effects, such as causing new parents to believe that if they read just one more book written by a leading expert on child rearing, they will miraculously turn into all-knowing perfect parents. Before our first child was born, my wife and I read six dozen parenting books. We felt compelled to gain more knowledge than a pediatrician with advanced degrees in child psychiatry, internal medicine, and nutrition. In turn, reading the books made us think we needed 1,154 baby gadgets to raise a child. We made the mistake of visiting one of the baby superstores, which have 35,000 square feet of products that play on the fears of new parents.

"Do you think we should buy this stuff that makes babies throw up if they've swallowed something poisonous?" I asked my wife. (After having three kids, I realize peas are cheaper and more effective.)

"I don't think we need that," she said. (She had fewer stop-the-clock-itis side effects than I did.)

"Look at this paint-by-number Sistine Chapel ceiling kit!" I said. "That sure would have been useful before we started the painting lessons."

I picked up a baby wipe warmer that plugs into a car's cigarette lighter outlet. I was convinced our new baby's life would be incomplete if we didn't purchase it.

"Are you sure we need that?" my wife asked skeptically.

"You're right," I said, "we'd better pick up the European outlet adapter kit, too, in case we take an emergency trip to France with our newborn."

It wasn't until our third child was born that I discovered we needed only one piece of equipment: a diaper. We got a free sample in the mail, so we were prepared. Everything else was optional.

Why use a baby wipe warmer when the wipes get warm if you leave them in the sun in your car? Why buy special baby cups, plates, and bowls when the food will end up on the floor? Just scatter the food on the floor to begin with. It's kind of like feeding chickens. A single feeding trough for all the kids works well, too.

Stop-the-clock-itis is exacerbated by the many other numbers during pregnancy—numbers that just don't add up. Let's begin with the number of visits to the doctor's office.

My wife had 162 doctor appointments during the final week before our youngest was born. During my wife's second trimester, her appointments were once per month. As her due date got nearer, the appointments switched to twice per month. During the ninth month, her appointments became weekly. But once her due date passed, it seemed as if her appointments were scheduled every fifteen minutes, with the sole purpose of each appointment being to schedule the next one. The problem with having appointments fifteen minutes apart is that you have to sit in the waiting room for twenty minutes before you're called in. It's impossible to know if they're calling you in late for your last appointment or early for your next appointment.

Then there's the number of books in the waiting room. Even though there are stacks of children's books, my son Paul asked me to read the same one every time. (I always accompanied my wife to her doctor appointments. That way, I could take care of Paul while she was busy with the doctor. Besides, the doctor gave away free lollipops.)

There are a lot of books to choose from in the waiting room, but Paul insisted on reading *The Lion King* every time. *Hakuna Matata* may mean "no worries and no cares," but the words send shivers up my spine as if I heard the sound of fingernails on a chalkboard. When Paul asked why Scar wanted to kill Simba, the only answer that came to mind was that Scar was forced to read the same book to Simba over and over again. I tried sliding the book under a chair cushion, but no matter where I hid it, it always appeared on the top of the book pile at our next visit. You'd think with all the advances in modern medicine, someone could develop a book that would remain interesting after the fiftieth time you've read it.

Sometimes stop-the-clock-itis spreads to others around the expectant parents. It caused some people to ask—every half hour—if my wife had our baby yet. These are people who are one taco short of a combo platter.

I usually give the question a pass the first time it's asked. But if it is asked again within an unreasonable amount of time, I respond, "Yes, she had the baby since you last asked. It took me three minutes to drive to the hospital, she had a five minute labor, I bonded with our new baby for eight minutes, and it took me fourteen minutes to get back because I hit some traffic." Then I give them a membership application to join the fertility police and say, "See you in the grocery store."

Even parents with more than two children can experience difficulties with math, although it takes a different form. These parents have trouble with this difficult math problem: "How many children do you have?"

Parents forget they have children. It's not that they want to forget, it's just that kids suck an enormous amount of thinking capacity out of your brain. The result is the inability to remember your kids' names and often if you even have kids. That's why I've created the "Rate the Risk That You're a Parent" quiz. I got the idea from Ken Pence of the Metro Nashville Police Department. Officer Pence—who is an actual police officer and not a member of the fertility police—created a great set of "Rate Your Risk" quizzes, including "Is someone going to break in and burglarize your home?" and "Are you going to be robbed, stabbed, shot, or beaten?"

When I took Officer Pence's "Rate Your Risk of Being Murdered" quiz, I was relieved to see I will live to meet my grandchildren. My high school guidance counselor must have been familiar with the quiz because he never once asked me to consider becoming a highly paid bank executive who moonlights as a fast food/liquor store clerk in a large city in an unstable foreign country, and is a gang-member who carries more than $2,000 cash in his wallet, and has recently terminated the employment of a handgun owner.

And I thought those career aptitude tests were a bunch of hogwash. It's clear they saved my life.

You might ask, "Isn't it obvious that you're a parent? You know if you have kids, don't you?"

That's an excellent observation since most moms and many dads were present at the birth of their children. I have a faint recollection of sitting next to a hospital bed in which my wife had complete authority over the television remote control for eighteen straight hours and I was forced to beg her to turn back to *Little House on the Prairie* so I could see if Michael Landon saved the neighbor girl who had fallen into a well. I even have a videotape of the experience. The episode of *Little House*, not the birth.

But, in my estimation, ninety-eight percent of parents forget that they have children. If you don't believe me, just look at the kids raiding the candy bin at the local grocery store checkout and the adults pretending those kids are someone else's progeny. My quiz will help jog your memory.

The following quiz rates the actual risk that you are a parent. The test uses known risk factors identified by adults who have been scientifically proven to have children. Don't panic if you have a high score. It could explain why the three-year-old raiding the candy bin looks exactly like you.

Check the box of each question that applies to you.

❏ **Is your minivan encrusted with so many Cheerios and Rice Krispies that when you hit a puddle it "snaps, crackles, and pops"?**

❑ Does your dining room set include six wooden chairs and one tall white plastic chair with an attached tray table covered with a layer of spaghetti sauce?

❑ Have you been awakened in the middle of the night by a call for "a glass of water" followed two hours later by a call for "dry sheets"?

❑ Did the most recent video you watched include talking vegetables, a train named Thomas, or a square sponge that wears pants?

❑ In public places, do complete strangers come up to you and say, "God bless you! I don't know how you do it!"

❑ Is every window in your home or apartment covered with fingerprints, mouthprints, and noseprints?

❑ Has your spouse ever asked, "Guess what *your* kids did!?"

❑ Have you yelled, "Stop making that noise!" while reading this chapter?

❑ Have you considered visiting your local health clinic for their $9.95 lobotomy special?

Score your quiz by counting the number of boxes you checked.

0—You probably aren't a parent. Retake the quiz in nine months.

1 to 5—Either you have kids or your neighbor has a large family and you left your back door open.

6 to 9—Botta bing, botta boom—you're a parent! You may even have more than one child. Wait until midnight and do a bed check to be sure.

After three children and many trips to the grocery store, my wife and I are as astute as CIA agents at hiding from the watchful eyes of the fertility police. And, with a record of three for three, I've perfected my expertise at determining the sex of a baby. But, with children, there are always new mysteries to be solved. For many of our friends with teenagers, the mysteries involve theft. That's why I'm working on a new quiz, "Rate Your Risk of Having Your Car Keys—As Well as Your Heart—Stolen by Your Children."

The Miraculous World of Potty Training

Within hours after becoming a parent you will notice your child's plumbing is defective. At first you may think this is a joke God is playing on you, since your baby appears to be a human dribble glass. No matter which way you hold him or her, you will get wet.

But God has an even better joke. At the same time a child is born, God blesses parents with the uncontrollable urge to catch their baby's spit-up before it stains the neighbor's new couch. God gets a big kick out of this. Your baby leaks and you feel compelled to dive like Willie Mays to make a catch that could be ESPN's play of the week.

There is a reason God designed babies to leak like a sieve. It gets parents to pray, usually eight to ten times per day—more often if they've fed their infant pureed prunes. And, it's a minor miracle when babies stop leaking.

Spit-up is one thing, diapers another. Each of the six dozen parenting books I read before our first child was born provided different advice on potty training. Some said to train a child by the time he or she was eighteen months old. Others suggested waiting until kids are three. Some recommended allowing the child to roam naked throughout the house during potty training. Others suggested dressing the child in pants but without a diaper. To save you some reading time, allow me to summarize by saying the main difference between these potty training techniques is whether you prefer to be frustrated by a clothed or naked child. The choice is yours.

I have personally developed several potty training methods that work quite well. The first is to schedule a business trip for the week when you plan to train your child. I found that potty training goes much smoother when I am eight hundred miles away in a quiet hotel room with a free movie channel and one of those small refrigerators stocked with expensive junk food. Unfortunately, this technique can only be used once before your spouse catches on, so alternate techniques are necessary for subsequent children.

Another technique is to purchase a few cases of the latest book on "how to toilet train your child in less then sixty minutes," then open them up and lay them carefully end-to-end across your family room. You won't actually learn anything from these books, but at least they'll keep "accidents" from staining your carpet. The local bookstore clerk may think it's odd when you ask for the cheapest book with the largest cover surface area, but since you're a parent, you're already growing accustomed to strange looks.

Books on topics other than toilet training work well too. I once purchased three cases of classic literature at a garage sale. It was a double bonus. First, it was a bargain.

Second, when someone asked how my two-year-old son was doing, I could honestly say he had been perusing Shakespeare earlier in the day. That really impressed people. What I didn't tell them was that he peed on *Macbeth* and didn't seem impressed with *The Taming of the Shrew* either. He may have a future as a book reviewer for *The New York Times.*

By far the most effective method of potty training is bribery. Most parents begin with M&Ms. It is best to have a pre-determined number of M&Ms you plan to give your child each time he or she uses the toilet successfully. Getting your child to use the toilet the first time is the most difficult, so the bribe needs to be a little larger than later on in the training. Also, as each day goes by without success, you will become slightly more anxious and want to increase the bribe because you cannot imagine one more hour of potty training. Here is a handy chart to use for rewarding your child during early training.

Day	Reward
1	Three M&Ms
2	Ten M&Ms
3	A small bag of M&Ms
4	A small bag of M&Ms and a Snickers bar
5	A two-pound bag of M&Ms and three Snickers bars

6   Thirty minutes of all-your-child-can-eat
        in the supermarket candy aisle

7   A bowl of pure cane sugar every morning
        for breakfast for a month

8   5,000 shares of M&M/Mars stock as well
        as everything else on this list

After you've purchased the stock for your child, you will have the following epiphany: "Changing diapers isn't as bad as I thought it was. Actually, changing diapers is kind of fun compared to toilet training. Besides, my child probably isn't ready for potty training yet. Maybe we can put this off for a while. Perhaps his professors can potty train him during his first year at college." You're already lowering your expectations. That's good!

The other question new parents have about potty training is when to stop bribing a child to use the toilet. This is a difficult question because most parents reward themselves with an M&M—or thirty—whether their child does his or her business or not. Subconsciously, this will train the parent to run for the candy dish every time the bathroom door creaks. This can prove embarrassing, especially when your daughter's prom date is sitting on the couch, your daughter mentions she has to use the bathroom before she leaves, and you feel compelled to stuff an entire Kit Kat bar into your mouth. That's why the final step to potty training your child is to join a twelve-step program for chocoholics.

Like it or not, while you're waiting for your child to be potty trained, you will have to change a diaper or two. Within a few months you will become an expert diaper changer with the ability to perform a one-handed change at midnight without turning on the lights. Your concentration will remain sharp because, for a sleepy parent, there's no smelling salt like a dirty diaper. But there is one place for which you will not be prepared to change a diaper—an airplane restroom.

In one of his most famous tricks, master escape artist Harry Houdini had his hands handcuffed behind his back, submerged his entire body in a large metal container filled with water—which was subsequently locked shut—and successfully escaped. While his trick was impressive, it pales in comparison to changing a diaper in an airplane restroom. I should know, because I consider that feat to be my most miraculous performance.

Most people don't believe me when I tell them about my feat. "Impossible," they say. These are people who think Elvis is still alive and believe Publisher's Clearinghouse will knock on their door any day now with a large check. While the magicians' code of conduct strictly forbids revealing how a trick is done, I am forced to publish my technique to clear my good name.

If you haven't been in an airplane restroom recently, let me begin by describing the accommodations. The airplane restroom makes a telephone booth feel like a forty-room mansion. The space is so small that when you face the door, it is actually behind you. For customer convenience, one of three messages appears on the bathroom door:

1) Vacant, 2) Occupied, or 3) Parent changing diaper inside, please contact *Guinness Book of World Records*.

Here's my secret technique. If after reading it you still don't believe it will work, try it for yourself. If you don't have a baby in your possession, feel free to borrow one from a fellow passenger.

Before entering the restroom, place a clean diaper on your head like a hat. Place one clean baby wipe behind each ear. These steps are critical because once diaper extrication begins it is impossible to pick up anything off the floor. In fact, it is impossible to pick up anything from the floor even if you're not changing a baby's diaper. I once used an airplane restroom that had two wallets, a Rolex watch, and an autographed picture of Babe Ruth on the floor. I'm sure they're all still there.

Next, put your foot in the sink. Carefully balance the baby on your knee with the baby's feet resting on top of the paper towel dispenser. Use your teeth to undo the diaper's adhesive tabs. With your right hand, shuck the diaper off the baby.

This procedure may cause your posterior to push the flight attendant call button. If an attendant knocks, shout through the door that you were just wondering if there was a movie on the flight. If the attendant persists, tell him or her to go away because you're just eight seconds off world-record pace.

Fold and seal the dirty diaper. Save it for later or drop it on the floor for future customers to enjoy.

Grab the wipes from behind your ears and clean the baby. If only one wipe is needed, remember to remove the other one before entering the main cabin. I once spent a weeklong vacation with a wipe behind my left ear.

Snatch the clean diaper off your head and apply to baby. Depending on the size of the infant, you may need to flip the child into the air using your knee. Usually four seconds of lift time is required to get the diaper under a twelve-pounder.

Remember proper hygiene. Like a mother cat, use your mouth to hold the baby by the scruff of the neck. Wash your hands.

If you've saved the dirty diaper, be assured that there is no good place to dispose of it in the plane. That's why it's convenient so many people sleep while flying. On the way back to your seat, gently place the present in an empty seat next to a sleeping passenger. If all seats are full, try the overhead bins.

If it weren't for the life-threatening nature of this trick, I would take my act to Las Vegas. I can hear the crowds gasping, "He's been in there too long—he'll never survive!" Just when they're beginning to think I'm dead, the restroom door would burst open and I'd triumphantly jump out—botta bing, botta boom—tossing the neatly-taped-shut diaper to a lucky audience member who will place it on her mantle as a keepsake. I think Harry Houdini would be proud.

Like most parents, I expected that after my kids were potty trained, I would experience the joy of newfound freedom. No longer would my hand be clasped around the handle of a diaper bag whenever I stepped out of the house. No longer would we need two shopping carts at the grocery store—one for food, the other for diapers. I eventually did enter the diaper-pail-free promised land. But I wasn't prepared for the language spoken there.

After my son was potty trained he moved immediately to potty talk. His favorite noun was "poop" and his favorite adjective was "poopy." When I say favorite, I don't mean he simply enjoyed using these words, I mean that he didn't let a sentence leave his lips without inserting one or the other. He also enjoyed telling us that anything poopy is disgusting.

This was a typical conversation:

Me: **Would you like me to read you a book before bed?**

Paul: **A poopy book?**

Me: **No, not a poopy book.**

Paul: **A poopy book! That's disgusting!**

Me: **I don't want you to say "poopy."**

Paul: **It's okay to say, "Annie pooped," isn't it?**

Me: **Yes, it's okay to tell me if Annie pooped.**

Paul: **Annie pooped. . . . That's disgusting!**

Me: **How do you know she pooped? She's asleep upstairs.**

Paul: **Maybe she pooped.**

Me: **Annie didn't poop.**

Paul: **She's not poopy?**

Me: **No. Why don't you pick a book to read.**

Paul: **A book about poop? That's disgusting!**

It didn't matter what the conversation was about, Paul could fit in his favorite word.

In song: "Old MacDonald had a farm, e-I-e-I-o. And on his farm he had some poop, e-I-e-I-o. . . . That's disgusting!"

In verse: "Hickory dickory dock, the mouse ran up the poopy clock. . . . That's disgusting!"

In prayer: "Please God, help Annie not to poop in her diaper. . . . That's disgusting!"

Once I took my kids camping along with a group of friends. There were a total of fourteen children under the age of five—kids who were allowed to pee in the woods whenever they wanted. One of my friends summed up a three-year-old boy's view of camping as, "the world is my toilet." (With any luck our kids will see the advent of space travel within their lifetimes. Then the entire universe can be their toilet.)

At one point during the weekend, a kid shouted out from behind a bush, "I peed on a woodchuck!" Paul quickly responded with, "Peed on a woodchuck! That's disgusting!" Paul didn't even know what a woodchuck was.

Paul, who was terrified to pee standing up in front of the toilet, lost his phobia in the great outdoors. He was particularly enamored with the idea of peeing in the water while swimming in the pond. I could tell he found it very convenient not to have to stop and interrupt his play. It was fine with me until he made the leap from peeing in the water to peeing whenever he was wearing his bathing suit. While building a sandcastle on the beach, he smugly announced, "I'm peeing, Dad."

I counted my blessings we weren't at the public swimming pool. There are always some kids who pee in the pool while swimming. I didn't want to have the first who peed in the pool while standing on the edge.

After many prayers—botta bing, botta boom—Paul stopped his potty talk. Within hours of being a parent, you notice your child's plumbing is defective. Thankfully, one day, you realize God is not only the God of Heaven and Earth but also of tongues and bladders.

Dad's Service Center, and Other Miracles of the Night

When God created Eve, he put Adam into a deep sleep. The deep sleep served two purposes. It kept Adam from feeling the removal of his rib. It also gave Adam the rest he would need, since he would soon be up all night with baby Cain and baby Abel.

Like Adam, I've worked the graveyard shift. My kids have a knack for calling me in the middle of the night and, for a while, I catered to their whims. But then I found a solution to my problem.

When I wake out of a sound sleep because one of my kids is calling for me, I no longer jump out of bed to see what the problem is. Instead—taking the lead from the major catalog merchants—I stay comfortably warm under the covers and shout back, "Thank you for calling Dad's Service Center. If you need a drink of water, press or say, 'one.' If you need to be escorted to the bathroom, press or say, 'two.' If you need. . . ."

When I hear, "Two! two! two!" then I know it is worth the effort to get out of bed.

This new policy is just one of the many ways I'm attempting to interact with my kids more like a business interacts with customers. I had to take this step because my daughter couldn't remember when Thanksgiving was.

One night I awoke to Maria's shouting. I made my usual dash to her bedroom, stumbling and bumping into things the entire way. When I reached her bedside, she had this dreadfully important query: "Is tomorrow Thanksgiving?"

Perhaps she thought she should be up making pies at the crack of dawn. All I knew was tomorrow wasn't Thanksgiving, she had no broken bones, and there wasn't a burglar in the house. My slumber had been interrupted for nothing. It was on my way back to bed that I decided to adopt business hours for my children. Here's how it works.

Businesses have long separated their customer service departments from their order-taking departments. You can call an 800 number, twenty-four hours a day, seven days a week, and order anything your heart desires. Just don't try to ask a question about a previous order—or anything else for that matter—or you'll be told to call the customer service department during normal business hours—nine to five, Monday to Friday. By coincidence, nine to five is also a time slot when I'm awake and free to answer questions about pending holidays.

So, when the kids call late at night, I respond to their pleas as long as they're ordering something. If they need a glass of water, a trip to the bathroom, or an extra kiss goodnight, I'll come running. But if they ask a non-order-related question, I simply shout back from my bed that they have to call back during normal business hours.

Don't get me wrong, I'm very pleasant when my kids are placing an order in the wee hours of the morning. In fact, since I've placed my share of catalog orders over the telephone, I know just what to say to make their ordering experience a pleasure.

> "Good evening, my name is Dad, how may I help you?"
>
> "I want a drink of water."
>
> "Could I get your zip code, please."
>
> "Dad, I just want a drink."
>
> "If you look on the back of your catalog, you'll see a promotion code beginning with the letter 'z' in the little yellow box."
>
> "Come on, I'm thirsty."
>
> "You might be interested in our other products that go quite well with water. For $1.99 we have a plastic cup that actually holds the water while you drink it. For $2.99 we have a glass mug, complete with handle to help keep you from spilling the water in your bed."
>
> "Dad, stop it. . . ."

> "For $29.95 we have a six-hour service plan
> for the glass of water. Should you need to use
> the restroom at any time during the night,
> we will escort you there at no additional
> charge."

My kids weren't thrilled with my new business hours, but they should be thankful I never instituted what I learned from the telemarketers who call our house at inconvenient times. I had considered waking them every half hour during the night to ask if they needed anything. You know, "Are you sleeping okay? Thirsty? Having any bad dreams? Want to know if tomorrow is Thanksgiving? Well it isn't, now go back to sleep."

The one shortfall of my business hours was that they didn't help me with the mythical creatures that visit my kids at night.

I've never been a big fan of creatures that break into your house at night to make deposits. It's not the gifts that I mind but rather the inevitable phone call saying that he/ she won't be able to make it this year.

"Hey, Tim, Easter Bunny here. I'm busy watching the NCAA basketball tournament and can't make it to your house tonight. You don't mind filling the kids' baskets again this year, do you?"

That made seven years in a row that the rabbit was a no-show and I got stuck filling the baskets. At least the Easter Bunny calls to say he's not coming. The Tooth Fairy never does, which is why I have to take the bus to work now.

It all started when Maria lost her first tooth. She heard about the Tooth Fairy from friends at school and wanted to place her newly freed incisor under her pillow to score some quick cash. Paul couldn't believe the concept: put a tooth under your pillow, wake up to money. He hadn't lost any teeth, but he figured the Tooth Fairy couldn't be too bright—paying for used teeth and all—so he grabbed an old toy truck and shoved it under his pillow.

During the night I made my rounds. It wasn't basketball season, but the Tooth Fairy was nowhere to be found. Maybe she was attending the National Dental Association's annual meeting in San Francisco—too far away to make a quick trip to our house.

Like the Tooth Fairy, I have a very special place for the teeth I collect. Myth has it that hers is a golden tooth-shaped box that can hold an unlimited number of teeth. Mine is a plastic bag on top of the microwave oven. I threw Paul's truck back into his toy box. Both kids were thrilled to find a shiny quarter under their pillows the next morning.

I wasn't prepared for the onslaught of questions that came at breakfast. "How did the Tooth Fairy get into the house? Don't we lock the doors at night? I can't find my doll, does the Tooth Fairy take anything else besides teeth? What's my truck doing back in my toy box? My friend from school says there's no Tooth Fairy and moms and dads replace the teeth—is that true?"

We've always taught our kids to be honest. This was one of those teachable moments that could shape our children for the rest of their lives. So I confessed.

"There is no Tooth Fairy," I explained ever so tenderly, so I wouldn't crush their youthful imaginations. "Does that make you feel sad?" I probed, hoping to ease the psychological scars that might be forming.

"Do we still get money?" asked Paul.

"Yes," I said.

"Then who cares!?" he smiled, holding the shiny quarter in his hand. We're still working with him on the concept of gluttony.

Now that my kids know I'm the Tooth Fairy, I'm held accountable for on-time delivery of quarters. When Maria lost her last tooth, I perpetrated the worst crime a parent can commit: I forgot to switch the tooth for the coin during the night. (Paul still hadn't lost any teeth, so he put a piece of broccoli under his pillow.) The next morning, I heard the yelps from their bedroom.

"Dad, you forgot to take the tooth!" they cried in unison. Thinking quickly, I shouted back, "Close your eyes and wait a minute!"

In the darkness of my bedroom, I grabbed a few coins off my bureau, dashed into their bedroom, removed the tooth and broccoli, and—botta bing, botta boom—escaped in a flash. Then, I cocked an ear to listen for my children's whispers of delight.

"He gave me two mint Lifesavers with lint on them," I heard Paul say.

"That's all?" asked Maria. "He gave me the keys to his car!"

Even after resolving the Tooth Fairy issue, one problem remained. My kids still got up too early in the morning. I was hoping the monsters could help straighten that out. I was wrong.

When my kids hadn't had any nightmares in a long time, I marched right up to their bedroom and dragged a small, hairy green monster and a large, two-headed beast out of the closet.

"What's the big idea?" I demanded. "When I was a kid you tormented me every night. You can't even make my kids whimper anymore."

"We don't dare come out when your kids are in the room," said the big one, hanging his two horn-covered heads sheepishly. "Your children scare us."

"They have no manners either," said the green one. "Whenever I try to growl, they interrupt me. Besides, the younger one sucks on his blanket and it's stinky."

"But, you're the monsters," I chided. "Aren't you supposed to be in control?"

"Look who's talking, Dad," said Mr. Two Heads. "I think we have about as much control as you do."

"I'm a strict disciplinarian," I protested.

"Sure you are," said Greeny. "Your three-strikes-and-you-get-a-punishment rule has worked wonders. You've given so many strikes you'll win the Cy Young Award this year."

"I think the three strikes rule has worked pretty well," I backpedaled. Thanks to my wife, I'm a champion backpedaler. I'm to backpedaling what Lance Armstrong is to the Tour de France. Unfortunately, monsters don't let matters drop that easily.

"The three strikes rule has worked great for your kids," said Greeny, running his eight fingers through the hair on his head. "We see what goes on around here. What about the other day when your boy made a tennis ball, videotape, cheese-melt sandwich in the microwave?"

"Oh, you saw that, did you?" I mumbled. "Well, I did give him a strike."

"Yeah, two more incidents like that and he might get a time-out," he laughed. There's nothing worse than being laughed at by a monster.

"Enough about me," I pleaded. "Can't you at least do something to scare them? Make your eyes glow in the dark perhaps?"

"I tried that once," said Mr. Two Heads. "Your son swatted my left head with a golf club. I was out of work for a week. My health insurance didn't even cover my doctor visits."

"Monsters have health insurance?" I gasped in disbelief.

"We didn't need it before we got the assignment in your kids' room," said Greeny. "You should see our premiums. They're even more frightening than your children."

"Why is it you want us to scare your kids, anyway?" asked Mr. Two Heads.

"I'm tired of them calling every five minutes, starting at 4 a.m., to ask if it's time to get up," I explained. "I have to convince them that monsters will eat them if they make any noise. You're not helping any. Can't you try harder?" I pleaded.

"Oh sure, like this is what I really wanted to do with my life," said Greeny. "During the day, when I'm not in your kids' closet, I go to college. I hope to work for the IRS some day. Now that's an organization that really knows how to scare people."

"Besides, have you ever listened to what your kids talk about before they go to sleep?" asked Mr. Two Heads. "The other night Paul asked Maria if animals' heads could come off the way Barbie dolls' heads do. After a comment like that, you think I'm sticking my head out from the closet?"

Now I'm afraid. Maybe they can make room for me in the closet. It will take a minor miracle to get me to come out. I wonder if Adam had the same problem with Cain and Abel?

It's a Miracle My Wife and I Are Sane (We Are, Aren't We?)

My wife and I often quote scripture to our children. My favorite verse to quote is from the Book of Acts, where Festus exclaims, "You are out of your mind, Paul!" I must have said the same thing to my son hundreds of times. But usually it's the parents who feel like they're losing their minds.

Before becoming parents, husbands and wives take many things for granted. These include free time, quiet meals, and sanity. While it's easy to identify when you've lost your free time and quiet, it is more difficult to determine the exact moment you lose your sanity. I pinpointed the loss of my sanity to somewhere between the birth of Maria and the day I looked out the window to see Paul out in the street wearing nothing but Teletubbies underwear and his sister's Cinderella glass slippers. In his defense, he called this his "golfing outfit," and he may have simply shanked a shot into the street. (He has an awful slice.) I'm sure he'll get a lot of media attention if he ever makes the PGA Tour.

These kinds of episodes smooth the rough edges off parents. If you're impatient, kids will wear you down until you begin to learn patience. If you like everything just so, your children will teach you to live with a little chaos in your life. Some days your kids smooth your rough edges with the gentleness of 120-grit sandpaper. Other days the smoothing feels more like you're a block of Parmesan cheese being grated.

When our daughter Annie was just about to turn one, she went through a difficult separation anxiety phase. Forget rough edges. Annie's separation anxiety made me feel like I was an old stump being chewed up by one of those huge stump-grinding machines. Annie cried when we put her to bed, when my wife left the room, and even when I left the room. Crying is not a common reaction when I leave a room.

But Annie didn't have a monopoly on anxiety. My wife and I have experienced a few anxieties of our own, even if they aren't of the separation variety. They're anxieties that have us questioning our sanity.

There's The-kids-haven't-eaten-anything-but-grilled-cheese-sandwiches-in-three-weeks anxiety and the If-I-have-to-read-*The-Cat-in-the-Hat*-again-I'll-scream anxiety.

I've suffered the There-was-a-ladybug-on-the-floor-a-minute-ago-but-now-it's-gone-and-the-baby-is-chewing-something anxiety. I've had a brush with Our-baby-looks-like-Blackbeard-the-pirate-my-son-is-missing-and-so-is-the-permanent-marker anxiety.

The I-can-hear-the-Talking-Barbie's-voice-but-it-sounds-like-it's-coming-from-underwater-and-I-just-heard-the-toilet-flush anxiety is no stranger to me. I've sweated through The-kids-picked-flowers-for-Mom-and-they-look-very-similar-to-the-ones-our-neighbor-planted-yesterday anxiety.

There was a Sunday when I sat through the Was-that-really-my-child-that-just-shouted-this-is-boring-right-in-the-middle-of-the-sermon anxiety. I was once forced to eat an entire box of candy at a friend's Christmas party after experiencing My-son-licked-one-of-the-chocolates-and-put-it-back-in-the-box-and-can't-remember-which-one-it-was anxiety.

When our kids started going to school there were a host of new anxieties. There was Our-first-grader-missed-a-spelling-word-and-we're-sure-her-chances-of-getting-a-college-scholarship-have-been-materially-reduced anxiety. I came down with I-hope-the-kids-in-my-son's-preschool-class-don't-teach-him-any-bad-habits-like-how-to-hotwire-a-car anxiety. There was also the corollary: I-hope-my-son-doesn't-teach-his-preschool-classmates-any-bad-habits-like-how-to-write-bad-checks anxiety.

These anxieties add up and cause parents to question their sanity, when what they should be questioning is the sanity of their children.

A friend of mine left her three-year-old son Joe at home with her husband. Her husband was trying to put up a fence in their yard while taking care of Joe. When she came home, this is what she heard.

"You're not going to believe what happened today. I left Joe in the house for twenty minutes to watch TV while I worked on the fence and—botta bing, botta boom—you'll be amazed at what he did. I came in the house to check on him and found the freezer door wide open with a chair standing in front of it. There's a line of melted Popsicle starting at the back door, running all the way through the kitchen and down the basement stairs, where I find Joe, naked from the waist down, opening a Popsicle with the fabric scissors. There are two empty Popsicle wrappers next to him and spots of melted juice all over the carpet around him. Can you believe that?"

Her response was, "Yes. In fact, I'm shocked he hadn't disassembled the computer and taken a swim in the toilet. Twenty minutes is an eternity to a three-year-old."

Since I've had a three-year-old boy, I'm quite aware of the damage that can occur in twenty minutes. I'm also familiar with the "insanity defense" used by young children. (We legal buffs like to call it *non compos mentis*, which is Latin for "Guess what my kids did?")

Little Joe was smart as a fox. Knowing that he would get in trouble for eating treats without permission, he deflected attention from his Popsicle violation by shucking off his pants, soiling the carpet, and wielding a sharp object. Had he fired up the chain saw, he could have gotten away with eating two cases of Twinkies and drinking an entire bottle of chocolate syrup. The insanity defense makes parents rejoice in the fact that their kids haven't injured themselves. What's a few dozen Popsicles here or there when your daughter has climbed out her bedroom window to slide down the roof on a toboggan?

Our kids use the insanity defense often, which has forced my wife and me to hone our legal skills. Sometimes our home sounds like a courtroom. We routinely subpoena Maria and Paul to the kitchen table so we can get to the bottom of things. I play the judge while my wife plays the prosecuting attorney.

Wife: **While your dad and I were upstairs getting ready for church, someone put a waffle in the VCR, turned the kitchen floor into a slip 'n slide, and filled my shoes with Cheerios. How do you plead?**

Paul objects: **We didn't add milk, so we were really good, right?**

Me: **Objection overruled.**

Paul: **You're oooie, Daddy. I don't like you.**

Me: **Pipe down or I'll hold you in contempt of court. Please continue, counsel.**

Wife: **Your honor, may I treat the witness as hostile?**

Me: **Yes. In fact, you may treat the witness as a child.**

Maria interrupts: **Paul, tell the truth. You did it. I saw you.**

Me: **Maria, you're badgering the witness and you're not even the prosecutor. Remember, your role is to break down in tears any moment now.**

Maria (blubbering): **Weeeeee bothhhhhh diiiiiiiiiid iiiiiiiiiiit. . . .**

Wife: **Why did you do it? Did my shoes look like cereal bowls?**

Maria (still blubbering): **I doooooon't knoooooow.**

Wife: **So you're pleading temporary insanity?**

Maria: **I guess.**

Paul: **I'm pleeting tempratary insanarpy too.**

Maria and Paul were sentenced to thirty minutes in their rooms. Because of previous convictions, they are serving concurrent terms, which brings their total room sentence to thirty-two years—thirty-one if they get time off for good behavior, which is impossible to imagine.

When my wife and I get tired of courtroom drama and want to see a movie, we don't have to leave home, as long as we're in the mood for a science fiction horror flick. I can almost hear the voice of that guy who narrates all the movie previews . . . "It's a story about a species that has human characteristics but isn't human. . . . It's a story about the conflict between humans and the savage beasts that rule the planet. . . . It's a story about heartless tyrants who treat humans as slaves. No, it's not the *Planet of the Apes* movie . . . it's *The Bete Family*."

It's uncanny how similar our home life is to the original *Planet of the Apes* movie, starring Charlton Heston. In the original film, three astronauts found themselves marooned on a strange planet where apes ruled and humans were mute animals. In our home, two parents find themselves marooned in a strange house where children rule and we are mute—or at least we can't get a word in edgewise.

It baffles me why Tim Burton spent $100 million to remake *Planet of the Apes* when he could have reshot the film in my home for under $100. We own a video camera. Hiring expensive make-up artists seems like a waste of money when allowing my kids to eat chocolate ice cream and rub their faces in our dryer's lint filter would produce a fine simian effect. Mr. Burton wouldn't even have had to spend money writing a script since the plot plays out naturally, day after day.

> *Scene 1*—**The Creatures Who Rule Our Lives. I arrive home from work, open the front door, and enter a world I don't recognize. When I left just nine hours earlier, the house had four walls and a floor. Now the four walls still exist, but they are connected by a sea of toys that extends out the back door and into the neighbor's yard. There is only one human being in sight. Except for the tormented look on her face, she looks vaguely familiar—almost wife-like. She sits mute on the couch with her head in her hands. I ask her how her day was. She glares.**
>
> **All of a sudden the silence is broken by a thunderous noise. The woman becomes terrified, screams, "They're back!" and hides behind the recliner. The noise sounds like a**

> pack of screaming monkeys beating on pots
> and pans while dragging a bed down the
> stairs. I look up to see a pack of screaming
> monkeys beating on pots and pans while
> dragging a bed down the stairs.

If you are under the age of eighteen, please stop reading immediately. The next scene is so graphic it should not be read by minors.

> There are two monkeys. The larger one
> is obviously the leader. The smaller one
> wields a golf club in one hand and holds a
> headless Barbie doll in the other. "Look!" he
> screams, "I made one of those things from
> the store!"
>
> "What things?" I ask, finding it
> unbelievable that I can hold a conversation
> with such a barbaric creature.
>
> "You know," he says, shoving the
> decapitated Barbie in my face, "One of those
> things with clothes but no head."
>
> "A mannequin?" I ask, disgusted.
>
> "That's it. I turned Barbie into a
> mannequin," he says proudly.

I am afraid to ask what he did with Barbie's head since it might cause the film to move from a "PG-13" rating to "R." I mentally make a note to hide Black Beauty and any other toy horses in the house so he can't play out a certain scene from *The Godfather*. I don't want him making me any offers I can't refuse.

The film continues with the typical chase scenes in which the woman and I attempt—unsuccessfully—to hide from the monkeys. They catch us and put us through hideous scientific experiments, such as asking the question "Why?" hundreds of times in a row.

> *Scene 2*—The Grand Finale. In the original movie's final scene, Charlton Heston rides a horse along a deserted beach. Off in the distance he sees half of the Statue of Liberty sticking out of the sand and screams as he realizes he is, in fact, on Earth. My homemade version would include a similar dazzling finale but without the high-budget props.

> As I sit on a large pile of dress-up clothes, I push aside a Cinderella dress to discover my favorite chair underneath. Realizing I am actually in my own home, I wouldn't scream—I'd tell the kids to wash the ice cream and lint off their faces, coax my wife out from behind the chair, and order a pizza for dinner.

Some people contend you will miss the days when your kids drove you insane. These people are called "grandparents." Just after your kids have used your briefcase to house the frogs they caught and filled their beds with sand so they could pretend they were sleeping on the beach, a grandparent will say, "You should treasure these moments because, before you know it, they'll be gone."

They must mean you'll miss your children after they've grown up, because it is doubtful you'll miss vacuuming up twelve pounds of sand or the fact that your laptop smells like algae. Grandparents may be right. My wife and I have good friends who learned this lesson when they sent their oldest child off to college. Watching them struggle with letting their daughter go made me realize that it's not just children who get separation anxiety. And that can make you yearn—just a little bit—for the good old days when the neighbor's flowers were missing and *The Cat in the Hat* had to be read for the thousandth time.

Ten Commandments Plus 672 Rules— If My Kids Obeyed It'd Be a Miracle

God had a great idea with the Ten Commandments. Rules help us understand what's acceptable and what isn't. Like most scripture, the Ten Commandments need to be interpreted for our time. That's why I've expanded "Honor your father and your mother" a little by adding 672 clarifying sub-rules. I didn't add them all at once; rather, as situations arose—and believe me, with our kids, situations arose.

My wife calls me the King of Rules, but I prefer the title Prince of Rules. The Bete family has a long, proud history of rules dating back to the late 1800s when an event occurred that made it unlikely I would ever own a member of the bovine family.

According to his obituary, William Henry Bete—my great, great, great grandfather—was killed by a cow. His death would have been respectable had he been trampled by a rodeo bull. At least that would have been easier to explain. But William was strangled to death by a black and white moo cow named Bessy.

William's obituary is sketchy, but this is the way I understand it. After an enjoyable dinner, Will was bringing his cow in from the field. The cow was in a "playful mood, running to and fro," the newspaper clipping reads. Somehow, the cow's rope leash tightened around William's midsection, constricting his bowel. Death ensued.

Before you ask, "Why didn't William simply move out of the way of the cow?" let me explain something. Today's cows are much slower than their nineteenth-century counterparts. In fact, it wasn't until 1905 that the cheetah surpassed the dairy cow as the world's fastest animal.

Perhaps if Will hadn't just eaten, he would have survived. His full stomach couldn't have helped his situation. That's why you should always wait twenty minutes after eating before walking your cow. Your life may depend upon it.

My mom also had a twenty-minute commandment for my siblings and me. Her rule was, "Wait twenty minutes after eating before swimming." During my childhood, I spent sixty-five days—in twenty-minute increments—sitting on the beach waiting for my food to digest. There must be something miraculous about twenty minutes because if you dip your toe in the water after nineteen minutes and fifty-eight seconds, you will curl up in a ball and instantly drown. This will occur even if all you've had to eat is a single cracker. Two seconds later, you'd be fine. And, whatever you do, don't take your cow swimming immediately after a big meal. That would be suicide.

Unlike Moses, to whom God dictated all Ten Commandments at a single sitting, God revealed rules to my parents one at a time over a period of many years. God may have wanted his wisdom to unfold slowly, but it is more likely because it was difficult for my bothers and me to inspire my parents with new commandments while we were grounded. God didn't need a burning bush to speak to my parents since he had us. (To be honest, God did reveal one commandment to my parents through a burning bush, but the commandment was "Keep matches out of reach of your children." Eventually the bush grew back.)

Two of my parents' favorite commandments were "No wild raccoons in the kitchen" and "Don't bring a live, flapping fish—still on the hook—into our bedroom to ask what kind it is." Some people mistakenly believe that the idea for locking automobile gas caps came from the major automobile manufacturers. In my opinion, my dad deserves the credit. My younger brother inspired him to create the commandment "Don't ever unscrew the gas cap on my car and fill the tank with water using the garden hose."

I won't tell you why my mom created the commandment "None of my sons may use shovels while I'm taking a nap." Let me simply say that, when motivated, two young boys can move five cubic yards of sand in about an hour.

Through our parents' new commandments, my siblings and I learned many innovative ways to "Honor our father and our mother." But none of us can use those same commandments with our children. It's unwise for parents to share their childhood commandments with their own children. Doing so puts bad ideas into your kids' heads. I have never told my children not to set our bushes on fire or to leave the raccoons outside. My kids haven't considered those activities—yet—and I don't want them to. Otherwise, they might end up like a childhood friend of mine who, whenever he saw a list of rules at a swimming pool, would ask, "How long do you think it will take me to break all of those?" Had the rules never been posted, he wouldn't have considered going down the slide backward, while spitting and holding a glass container. His record for being asked to leave was four minutes.

But for new parents a starter set of commandments is very useful. The starter set doesn't include all the specifics but provides a foundation from which to build their own commandments.

First there is the greatest commandment for children: "Stop that." All other commandments are derived from "Stop that." The commandment "Quiet down" can be translated "Stop that noise." "Sit still" can be translated as "Stop that fidgeting." Even when you are not in the same room with your children, it is useful to yell, "Stop that!" every fifteen minutes or so. Nine out of ten times, your children will respond, "Okay," which just proves that they were up to no good in the first place. On the odd occasion when they respond, "We weren't doing anything," you can always follow up with "Yeah, but you were thinking about doing something." This will convince your children that you can read their minds, which is a useful thing for you to have them think.

When it comes to creating new commandments, some parents are better than others. Even the best commandment-makers occasionally find that they are too tired to create new regulations. That's when *Tim's Random Commandment Generator* (patent pending) comes in handy. Here's how it works. Pick one item from each column and—botta bing, botta boom—instant commandment! (Make sure to mix and match.)

Column 1	Column 2	Column 3
Never	take candy	from a stranger
Always	look both ways	before crossing the street
Always	say your prayers	before going to bed
Never	touch the animals	at the zoo
Always	pick up your toys	before eating dinner
Always	wash behind your ears	when taking a bath

Most parents tell their kids to wash their hands before dinner and not to touch the animals at the zoo. But with my handy random rule generator, you'll be spouting off commandments such as, "Never wash behind your ears before crossing the street" and "Always touch the animals before eating dinner." That will keep your kids on their toes.

My love for commandments is why I admire airlines so much. They have a lot of rules, and I have even adapted some for home use. For example, if you don't get on the plane after the first boarding call, the flight attendant pleasantly provides three more announcements before the final boarding call. After the final boarding call, however, you may be locked out of the plane.

When I call my kids to dinner the first time, they know there will be subsequent calls and they don't need to rush. However, if they arrive at the table after my final call, I tell them they have missed their meal and they will have to wait three hours for the next one, which will be served in terminal B.

As stringent as the airlines are with their rules and regulations, I was pleased to discover that they can be as quirky and inconsistent as I am.

Several years ago, the Federal Aviation Administration (FAA) investigated the flight of a 300-pound Vietnamese pot-bellied pig with a pink bow on its tail. The FAA concluded that the airline acted "reasonably" when it allowed the pig to fly. Not even I am that reasonable.

According to the FAA, the pig was registered as a "therapeutic companion pet" for its owner, who suffered from a heart condition and claimed to need the pig to relieve stress. Airline regulations permit "therapeutic companion pets" and don't rule out the possibility that the pet is made of "the other white meat." Personally, sitting on an airplane for six hours with a 300-pound pig wouldn't be a stress reliever for me, unless the pig was a masseuse or at least a good conversationalist.

The pig owner reported her pet weighed thirteen pounds when she made the reservation. (Seems the pig gained 287 pounds between then and the time the flight took off.) Airline employees in Philadelphia, where the flight originated, let the weight discrepancy slide. These are the same employees who would reject your bag if it were two ounces over the twelve-pound maximum weight limit. The live pig gets a clear pass. A bag made of pigskin would have been rejected.

But not all passengers had their stress relieved by having a swine aboard. The 300-pound pig, whose name is being withheld to protect its identity, slept for most of the six-hour flight from Philadelphia to Seattle. An airline report stated, "As the Boeing 757 landed with 200 passengers, the pig awoke, tried to barge into the cockpit and stormed into the galley." According to the *Philadelphia Daily News*, "Witnesses reported it squealed wildly and left steamy droppings on the airport carpet and inside an airport shuttle van." That's when the incident escalated to a new level of severity. The FAA strictly prohibits leaving steamy pig droppings unattended in an airport shuttle van. Several terrorist groups tried to take credit for the incident.

What was the pig owner's response to all of this? The same one my kids give when they've broken a rule. She denied any involvement. Even with 200 witnesses, the pig's owner denied that her porky pet ran around the aircraft willy-nilly.

While speaking to a reporter for the *Philadelphia Daily News*, the owner shouted, "My pig did not run around the plane's aisles. My pig did not run around anywhere. Print that in the *Daily News*." They did, which is why I can reprint it here.

The same airlines that have twelve pages of regulations describing the penalties for giving an extra bag of snack mix to a passenger provide no rules for curbing a disruptive pig. The kicker was that the pig was allowed into first-class for free. I bet they didn't even check to see if it had enough frequent flyer miles for the upgrade.

I've always said I wouldn't relax any of the 672 commandment sub-rules for my kids until pigs fly. Maybe it's time to make a few changes.

Whether they're my rules or the airlines', some kids are just too smart for their own good. When Maria started learning American history in school, she became very patriotic, which was enough to make me want to secede from the union. Don't get me wrong. I love this country. We fly a flag outside our front door. I always vote—twice if I can get away with it. But Maria began reliving history and made life awfully uncomfortable at our house.

After hitting her brother and being ordered to her bedroom (commandment sub-rule #137), she glared and shouted, "This is America where anyone can do what they want! You can't boss me in America!"

Since I still had a few parenting books left over from potty training, I looked up how to handle such an outburst. (It was in the chapter on "childhood mutiny.") I quickly hid the phone book so she couldn't find the number for the American Civil Liberties Union. She hadn't declared whether she was liberal or conservative, but I wasn't taking any chances. I unplugged all our telephones too. I didn't want to be driving down the street listening to Rush Limbaugh and hear my daughter's voice.

Maria: **"Mega dittos, Rush. I'm a first-time caller, long-time listener. I've been sentenced to sixty-two days in my room for hitting my brother. Could you tell me if this violates the Bill of Rights?"**

Rush: **"Sounds like a left-wing conspiracy. I wouldn't be surprised if being sent to your room isn't another Democratic cover-up."**

Actually, the cause of my daughter's newfound patriotism was the American Girl dolls—more specifically, the books that help sell the dolls. I'd been reading her the book about Felicity who lived in Virginia in 1774. Felicity's father owned a store and decided not to sell tea because he believed the King's tax was unjust. Two chapters later—botta bing, botta boom—there's anarchy in our house.

The Declaration of Independence listed about thirty ways that the King of England was depriving colonists of their rights. Maria's list was much longer.

According to Maria, it is quite unfair that she must bathe. She finds eating most vegetables morally reprehensible. A set bedtime? Preposterous. Wearing shoes out of doors? Shameful.

I don't mean to curtail her "pursuit of happiness" . . . wait a minute, that's exactly what I intend. After all, a man's house is his castle, and last time I checked, castles are where kings live. At least her baby sister Annie is still a loyalist.

A king can't be too careful, though. I may make the rules, but I'm on the lookout for revolutionaries. I could have sworn I heard someone yell, "The parents are coming! The parents are coming!" when I came home from work the other day.

Paul is interested in the Boston Tea party too. I know I should be excited and support him in his love for history, but instead I hid all our coffee. We don't drink tea, and I don't want to find our bathtub awash in coffee grinds and filters. Besides, I made him pay for a picture he broke, and I think I heard him mumble something about taxation without representation.

I feel the inspiration for a new commandment coming on.

The Parable of the Dirty Laundry, and Other Miraculous Lessons

While commandments help train your children, parables can work wonders too. Of course, today's parents run into some problems that Jesus' parables didn't cover. If you revise the parables slightly, your children will better grasp your point.

Last summer I couldn't get my kids to bring their things inside after playing in the backyard. Rather than scold them, I gathered my children around me and told the parable of the dirty laundry.

> *Hear this! One day, a child was playing outside. As the day grew warmer, the child began to remove layers of clothing.*
>
> *As he disrobed, a sweatshirt fell on the path, where his parents had to pick it up.*
>
> *A T-shirt fell on rocky ground, where his parents had to pick it up.*
>
> *Some socks fell among thorns, which really upset his parents because they had to go into the thorns to retrieve the socks.*

> *Finally, when the child came inside and got*
> *ready for bed, his remaining clothes fell into the*
> *dirty clothes hamper—probably by accident—*
> *and his parents were exceedingly happy.*

"Why didn't the parents put a hamper in the backyard?" asked my puzzled children. "Or buy the kid new clothes? We don't understand this parable, please explain it to us."

"The children are you," I explained. "I want you to bring your things in with you when you come inside after playing. Then, the clothes that fall in the hamper will bear fruit and yield a hundred or sixty or thirtyfold, until we're forced to do laundry because we have nothing left to wear."

"Do you have any more wisdom for us?" my children asked.

"As a matter of fact, I do," I said. "Try this parable on for size."

> *As the youngest child came back from buying*
> *a Popsicle at the ice cream truck, she fell victim*
> *to her elder sister, who stole her sibling's*
> *Popsicle and ran and ate it in the tree house.*
> *The youngest child sat, crying, on the side of*
> *the road.*
>
> *The youngest child's brother walked past*
> *eating his own Popsicle but would not share it*
> *with his sobbing, Popsicle-less sibling. Likewise,*
> *the youngest child's other brother came by,*
> *eating his Popsicle, but would not share it*

with his Popsicle-less sibling. He even taunted the youngest child, saying "Nah, nah, I have a Popsicle and you don't."

But a middle-aged man came upon the youngest child and was moved with compassion at the sight, chased down the ice cream truck, and bought the child another Popsicle. Then the middle-aged man lifted the child on his shoulders and carried her to where the rest of the family was gathered.

Which of these, in your opinion, was the child's father?

"You can't prove I took Annie's Popsicle," stammered Maria.

"I wish you drove an ice cream truck," said Paul. "Hey, if we get Popsicle juice on our sweatshirt, do we still need to bring it inside?"

"Whoever has ears to hear ought to hear," I said. (Not that my children have ears.)

In the parable of the prodigal son, the younger son took half his father's estate and spent it on extravagant luxuries. He was wasteful to say the least. My son, on the other hand, could stand to be a little more prodigal.

Paul collects everything—leaves and pinecones, sticks and pebbles, bottle caps and dead bugs. One of the reasons he collects so many things is that he was taught the concept of recycling by his preschool teachers—and for that I will never forgive them. He believes so strongly in recycling that we are no longer allowed to throw away anything. Paul has mastered the premise that recycling means making something into something else. He has trouble with the concept that the something else should be more than a plastic juice bottle glued to an empty tissue box.

"Look, Dad!" he says, "I recycled these!"

"What is it?" I ask cautiously. The last time Paul recycled something, I became the proud owner of a Popsicle-stick, used-adhesive bandage tie clip. It may have even been a Popsicle stick once used in a parable.

"Can't you tell?" he asks, rolling his eyes. "It's a plastic juice bottle glued to a tissue box." He holds up an object that looks like the Stanley Cup trophy if it were co-sponsored by Gerber and Kleenex.

"What will you do with it?" I inquire, backing away.

"I'll put it right here, on the kitchen table, so everyone can see it," he says, beaming.

Now we have the Gerber/Kleenex Stanley Cup for a centerpiece. I look on the bright side and imagine that I'm eating dinner in Wayne Gretsky's dining room.

Paul's recycling is getting to be a problem. He is to paper towel roll tubes what Imelda Marcos is to shoes. We have so many paper towel roll tubes that—if you put them end to end—a gerbil could run from our house in Ohio to Brazil without ever seeing daylight. I could prove it too, but Paul won't let me touch his collection.

I wouldn't mind the paper towel roll collecting as much if Paul waited until all the towels had been used before taking the roll. The way he shucks off the sheets leads you to believe he thinks they're just packaging to keep the cardboard tube from getting damaged.

As I consider the possibility of using the Stanley Cup centerpiece as a vase, Paul takes a plastic shopping bag and "recycles it" by slipping his arms through the handle holes so that the bag is on his back.

"Look, Dad! I'm Buzz Lightyear!" he shouts, flying around the room with a plastic bag for a rocket pack. I look on the positive side: Maybe he can get a job doing wardrobe for low-budget movies. (He could even help with the next *Planet of the Apes* sequel since he'll also star in it.) I'll save fifty dollars on his birthday present, too, by giving him a brown paper bag and telling him it's a "Woody the Cowboy" costume.

If Paul doesn't have an immediate use for an item, he hides it in one of his many lock boxes. If it's good enough to hold the Social Security Trust Fund, it's good enough for old buttons, pieces of string, and expired grocery store coupons. (Some economists predict that Paul's collection of expired coupons may be worth more than the Social Security surplus in a few years.)

While most of Paul's recycling collections consist of ordinary household items, he does have some treasures. "Treasures" are items that have been processed by our automatic treasure-making machine. You place any ordinary object in the hole in the top, press the start button, wait fifteen minutes and—botta bing, botta boom—the object magically transforms into a priceless bauble. Our treasure-making machine washes clothes too. Very convenient.

I'm getting used to the concept that what is garbage to me is beautiful to Paul. As the saying goes, "Beauty is in the eye of the beholder." Or, in Paul's case, "Beauty is in the eye of the paper towel roll holder."

Paul is frugal with his monetary treasure too. His money-management abilities emerged at an early age. It was clear by age two that Maria would be an actress. She's a drama queen and can make the removal of a Band-Aid look like a Shakespearean death scene. It was also clear that, if Maria succeeds on the Broadway stage, Paul will own the theater in which she acts.

At four years old, Paul was probably the only kid in America who read *The Wall Street Journal*. I'm kidding, of course. He couldn't read at four, so he made me read it to him. Paul has the mind of an accountant. His money-mindedness started innocently enough. When he was two, he began asking for some of the change when my wife and I were buying things. A penny here, a nickel there. Then, two years later, I found Paul counting his pile of coins.

"I have 102 dollars," he said.

I thought it was cute that he was pretending to count his money. Then I noticed that he was putting the quarters in piles of four.

"How did you know that four quarters make a dollar?" I asked.

"Mom told me," he said. "Ten dimes make a dollar too."

"What are you going to do with all that money?" I gasped.

"Keep it," he said. "I'm going to keep it."

That's the same answer he gave when his preschool teacher asked him what he would do if he found a pot of gold. While the other preschoolers were busy imagining the candy and toys they would buy with their pots of gold, Paul was saving for retirement.

Paul didn't keep all of his coins. He decided to invest in real estate. Unfortunately, the real estate was our house.

One day when I came home from work, Paul said, "See my new desk."

"That's Mom's desk," I corrected.

"It's mine now," Paul said. "I paid her ten dollars for it."

That's what I get for leaving my wife without any money. I'm just glad she didn't sell my computer to him.

Paul's banking proficiency has made it difficult for us to teach him the concept of giving alms to the poor. Our family has a cardboard box in which we put a quarter each time we skip a snack or dessert. The money we collect, we give to the poor. Paul's implementation of our program would have impressed even an Enron executive.

"I get to put a quarter in the box," Paul said on the first day we put the box out.

"What did you give up?" I asked.

"I gave up a snack," he said.

"What snack? I just saw you finish a bag of pretzels."

"I didn't eat any ice cream," Paul answered.

"We don't have any ice cream," I said.

"But, if we did, I wouldn't have eaten it, so I ate pretzels instead," Paul justified. "I get to put in a quarter for not eating the ice cream we didn't have."

"You didn't eat any cookies either," I added sarcastically.

"Thanks for reminding me," he said. "I'll put two quarters in the box."

After realizing Paul's logic was superior to mine—and having run out of parables to tell him—I decided to turn to *Poor Richard's Almanack* for some human wisdom to share with my offspring. *Poor Richard's Almanack* was written in what children refer to as the pre-VCR era—sometime around when dinosaurs roamed the Earth. They may think the book was titled *Poor Richard's* because Richard was a poor speller (everyone knows that "almanac" doesn't end in "k"). What children haven't learned is that people used to spell words differently—take, for example, "Ye Olde Malt Shoppe," from the *Archie* comic strip. Unfortunately, today's kids have no idea who Archie is and think he must have lived with Poor Richard and the dinosaurs.

Lucky for us, Ben Franklin's wisdom applies as much today as it did when he was tragically eaten by a T-Rex while trying to invent fire. Mr. Franklin said, "A spoonful of honey will catch more flies than a gallon of vinegar." That's a good thing to know if you need to catch flies. Ben even provided advice for those of us who aren't enamored with catching bugs. For example, the proverb "An empty bag cannot stand upright" is a good response the next time the cashier asks, "Paper or plastic?"

Since I did so well with parables, I thought I'd translate a few of Ben's proverbs so my children could understand them easier. For starters, we'd need a catchier title—something that resonates with my children's experience.

Perhaps *Old, Pale, Flabby Dad's Almanac* or *Poor, Poor, Sad and Pitiful Dad's Big Book of Advice*. While those titles are technically accurate, they wouldn't catch my kids' attention. Better call it *101 Secrets for Beating Video Games* so the kids will actually read it.

"The early bird gets the worm" is best translated as "The first one out of bed gets the last Pop-Tart." "He's a fool that makes his doctor his heir" is clearer as "He's a fool that lets his sister hold his ice cream cone while he goes to the bathroom." "Little strokes, fell great oaks" is nice but "Change little folks, when their diapers are soaked" is more practical advice.

Ben Franklin wrote other proverbs that simply need to be expanded a bit. "A good example is the best sermon" is a nice thought, but what Ben left out was, "The best sermon is less than ten minutes long so you can beat the rush to buy donuts after church."

Ben also said, "Early to bed, early to rise, always makes a man healthy, wealthy, and wise." What Ben forgot to mention was once you are a parent, you will want to go to bed early but will be up all night with the baby and have to rise early whether you want to or not.

My wife is skeptical of Ben's proverbs.

"The doors of wisdom are never shut," I quote.

"Neither is our back door," she complains, "and flies are coming in."

"See," I say, "Ben was right about the honey. And, since the door is already open, maybe we can get the kids to go outside and pick up their clothes."

The Miracle of Parent-Child Communication

Saint Paul wrote, "One who speaks in a tongue should pray for the power to interpret." Sometimes I feel like I'm speaking in tongues and my children aren't able to interpret. Perhaps I need to pray harder for my children to understand me. I'm sure they're praying for me to understand them. I recently found out the firefighters in our town need some prayers too.

In a nearby preschool, a local firefighter was teaching fire safety to three- and four-year-olds. One of his first questions was, "What do you do if your clothes are on fire?" Instantly, one of the kids shouted out, "Close your closet door!" Answers like that make it difficult to continue a presentation.

Had I been the instructor, I would have clarified the question by asking, "What do you do if the clothes *you are wearing* are on fire?" I'm confident that one of the dear little ones would have responded, "Why would you put on clothes that were on fire?" At that point I would have hopped into my fire engine and gone home. Having to teach fire safety to preschoolers is only one reason I am not a firefighter. I also prefer to work in an office that is less than 1,000 degrees.

Firefighters aren't the only ones who have difficulty communicating with children. Parents do too, but only on the days that end in "y." The subtleties of the English language are often lost on youngsters. So, when you are talking with your children, be as specific as possible. Otherwise, your kids will think you are even crazier than you actually are.

For example, one day after your son has rollerbladed on the roof of your car, used your credit card to purchase a pet boa constrictor, and tied his sister to a telephone pole, you are giving him a good talking to. He isn't paying attention to you, and you're incredibly frustrated, so you segue into a question about personal grooming tools. Or at least that's the way he hears it.

"Do you know what the other side of a hairbrush is for?" you ask sternly. Your son looks at you like your brain has blown a gasket.

In my youth, during the heat of a reprimand when my parents asked me a question to which I didn't know the answer, I had two choices. Tell them to check in our *World Book Encyclopedia* (which is what they told me to do when I asked a difficult question), or keep my mouth shut and hope that they would forget the question and get back to my behavior. I always opted for number two, which is why I am still alive today.

Now, your son will inevitably discuss your level of sanity with his friends, who will share their parents' looniness. One of his friends will disclose that his father—

right in the middle of chewing him out for breaking a window—claimed that he could do tricks with clothing accessories. Specifically, he said, "I can use my belt for other things besides holding up my pants!" Much to the child's dismay, his dad did not proceed to juggle his belt along with a bowling ball and flaming torch.

Perhaps you don't believe in discipline techniques that involve personal grooming tools or clothing accessories. Many experts on child rearing would agree that spanking is never an appropriate discipline technique. These are experts whose kids have never flushed their wallets down the toilet just to see if they would fit.

Nonetheless, you may still experience communication gaps with your children. Our kids are masters of confusion. One day, when Paul was three, my wife was driving home from a shopping trip with him in the back seat. "What were you looking at?" Paul asked his mom.

"When?" she asked.

"You were looking at *when*!?" Paul questioned indignantly, as if "when" was some noun that my wife had been forbidden to gaze upon.

"When was I looking at what?" she tried to clarify in vain.

"Yes, when were you looking at what?" he volleyed.

That's why it's safer to drive a car while talking on a cell phone, drinking a sixty-four-ounce soda, and knitting an afghan than to drive with a single three-year-old in the vehicle.

But my wife isn't the only one who gets to enjoy Paul's psychobabble. At breakfast one morning, when I asked him what he wanted to eat, he decided to provide me with only the first letter of his desire. What fun! He learned this trick from watching us help his sister sound out words.

"A," he croaked incessantly. "A . . . a . . . a . . . a . . . a . . . a. . . ."

Finally, in frustration, I began to blurt out guesses in machine-gun style.

"Apple? Apricot? Artichoke? Asparagus? Almond? Adzuki bean?" I blurted.

"A . . . a . . . a . . . a . . . a . . . a. . . ." he continued.

Perhaps it wasn't food that he wanted after all.

"Accordion? Anthill? Aardvark? Appalachian Trail? Albatross? Alpaca?" I continued in a single breath.

Ten minutes and twelve pages of the *Webster's New Collegiate Dictionary* later, I gave up.

"It was apple juice," he finally conceded. "Pretend apple juice for my stuffed dog."

"A . . . a . . . a . . . a . . . a. . . . " I began.

"What do you want, Daddy?"

"Aspirin or amnesia," I confessed. "Either will do."

Experts on interpersonal communication say that all communication requires a sender and a receiver. Don't let this discourage you. Your children are unlikely to willingly receive anything you say. At times, you will have more luck talking to your dog than your kids. Nonverbal communication skills help bridge the gap with your non-listening child. Eye rolling is a particularly useful way of communicating how you feel. So is that shocked look of disbelief you can only achieve when you first see your child drawing a picture with markers on your new white tablecloth. Blowing steam out your ears like a cartoon character is also useful—if you can do it—but turning red as if your head were full of steam is equally effective.

It may take more than an aspirin to cure the communication headaches caused by your children. Rather than encourage your children to talk, I recommend encouraging them to listen. Kids will learn to talk without encouragement. Listening is another story.

Sure, kids can pass their hearing tests at school, but that's because the test consists of raising your hand when you hear a beep or buzz. Because their hearing is still developing, children are only able to hear certain frequencies, none of which include those made by a parent's voice. If the same hearing test were administered replacing the beeps and buzzes with statements such as "Time for bed" and "Stop hitting your sister," all kids would test as completely deaf.

Communicating with our youngest daughter is more my speed. When Annie was just beginning to talk, she got by quite nicely with a one-word vocabulary—the word "umm." Usually "umm" meant yes. And when you only have a single word in your arsenal, you use it to answer every question. You've heard of "yes men"? Annie was an "umm girl." Annie would have made a great expert witness, regardless of the topic.

Prosecutor: **"Is it correct that you're an expert in the field of ballistics?"**

Umm.

Prosecutor: "**Is this the gun used in the robbery?**"

Umm.

Prosecutor: "**Are you one hundred percent sure?**"

Umm.

(Unfortunately, Annie didn't hold up under cross-examination.)

Defense attorney: "**Are you a water buffalo?**"

Umm.

Defense attorney: "**Have you ever lived on Mars?**"

Umm.

Defense attorney: "**Is Britney Spears talented?**"

Umm.

Annie became more adept at using "umm" to mean different things. If she snapped her teeth together while umm-ing, "umm" meant "yum." This simple trick allowed her to communicate as well as a *New York Times* food critic. Since Paul's potty training episodes qualified him as a *New York Times* book critic, perhaps they can share an office together someday.

One day, as we rolled through town in our minivan, Annie cleansed her palette with Cheerios and grape juice while commenting on the delicacies of each restaurant we passed. Only the finest establishments got the coveted five-umm rating.

Krispy Kreme Donuts got four umms for its heavy use of sugar and free hats. Wendy's Restaurant got three umms for its Jr. Bacon Cheeseburger. As we drove past the local garden center, Annie belted out a rare five-umm salute, and I felt a Cheerio pelt the back of my head.

"They give away free popcorn," my wife explained. "She wants you to stop."

I sighed with relief. I was afraid Annie was eating mulch again.

Even with her one-word vocabulary, it wasn't difficult to imagine Annie speaking in complete sentences. Maria went straight from "goo" to six-hour monologues. Now I have to brace myself before asking, "What did you do at school today?"

"I brought in the bird I made out of a paper towel tube and Olivia said it was great but Karen liked Elizabeth's bird better than mine and Bobby made a really disgusting noise and I told him it was disgusting but he just laughed and I was the only girl wearing a jumper today but I didn't mind because I love jumpers—why do they call them jumpers anyway?—oh, yeah, Jane was wearing a jumper, so I wasn't the only girl wearing one, there were two of us—Jane and me—but her jumper was a different color. . . ."

Eventually oxygen masks drop from the overhead compartments because all the air has been sucked out of the room.

Paul, on the other hand, makes a Vermont farmer sound verbose.

"What did you do at school today?" I ask.

"Work," he says.

Then, one day, Annie uttered the sound I'd been longing to hear—"da." "Da" quickly multiplied into the multi-syllabic—"da da." Botta bing, botta boom—I was elated.

"Do you love Da Da?" I asked.

"Ummm," she said. And I'm sure she meant "yes" because I wasn't even holding any popcorn.

Now that's communication.

Five Loaves,
Two Fish—What, No Tartar Sauce?
(or, My Son Ate a Vegetable—It's a Miracle!)

You can look almost anywhere in the Bible and see that eating can be a religious experience. There was the Last Supper, of course, and the multiplication of loaves and fish. John the Baptist dined on locusts and wild honey, and the Israelites ate manna in the desert. Except for that fruit incident in the Garden of Eden, most of the food experiences in the Bible were positive. That's because they involved adults—not children—eating food.

If you imagine yourself on the hillside when Jesus multiplied the five loaves and two fish to feed more than 5,000, I think you'll see my point. There must have been a thousand children present. By my calculation, immediately after the miracle, 400 kids would have said they "didn't like fish." Three hundred and fifty children would have complained that their "bread was touching their fish," and therefore they couldn't eat it. One hundred and fifty kids would have whined that the fish was "inedible without tartar sauce." Seventy-five would have asked for "fish sticks instead of the whole fish." Finally, twenty-five children must have dropped their fish on the ground and cried because it was dirty, even though they never would have eaten it in the first place.

I could be wrong, but that's what would have happened if my kids were on that hillside. Because Jesus was in charge, however, two miracles occurred. First, he multiplied the loaves and fish. Second, all the kids ate it. You decide which was the greater miracle.

Although we're far from biblical times, eating with your children can still be a religious experience, and you may even see a miracle now and then. Like many other areas of child development, learning to eat comes in stages. It is normal for your toddler to throw food. That's why it is a normal stage of parent development to wear food. Feeding your children will help you pass through nine stages of parent development. Recognizing these stages in advance can reduce the stress felt by new parents. It will also help parents appreciate the miracle that happens when a child actually eats something.

Stage 1, birth to nine months. Mothers begin to feel like a twenty-four-hour, mobile restaurant with a very limited menu. Fathers learn that baby formula smells awful.

Stage 2, nine to twelve months. Parents learn to pick up spoons and dishes off the floor as well as bugs out of their child's mouth. Parents also develop ability to clean yogurt off the cat.

Stage 3, twelve to eighteen months. As the child's aim becomes more accurate, parents learn to dodge meatballs and also how to clean spaghetti sauce off the ceiling fan.

Stage 4, eighteen to twenty-four months. Parents learn that putting the toddler's plate at another family member's place—and telling the toddler not to touch it—is the most effective way to get the child to eat. During this stage, the child learns to ricochet food off a cabinet to hit the cat. Parents gain skills in vacuuming pieces of hot dog out from behind sofa.

Stage 5, two to three years. As the child learns to toss an Oreo into a sibling's mouth from across the table, parents learn to catch Oreos in mid-air. The child learns to hold a glass. Parents learn not to cry over spilled milk.

Stage 6, three to four years. The child learns to use a fork. Parents learn first aid for puncture wounds caused by forks. The child is able to pour from a small pitcher. Parents are able to clean maple syrup out of siblings' hair.

Stage 7, four to five years. The child is interested in where food comes from and asks many questions. Parents explain where food comes from and lose the desire to eat sausage.

> **Stage 8, five to twenty-two years.** The child consumes enormous quantities of everything in sight causing the parent to make multiple trips per week to the supermarket.
>
> **Stage 9, age twenty-two+.** The child is forced to buy groceries and cook for himself or herself after graduating from college. The parent learns to always set an extra place for "drop-in" guests.

While I understand the stages of child and parent development, I still worry that my kids aren't eating enough chocolate and French fries. Their butter and ketchup intake is on the low side too.

Actually, I'm not worried about these things, but several leading food manufacturers are. That's why they've invented chocolate French fries, green ketchup, and blue and pink squeeze margarine. No kidding.

Personally, I've never had to tell my kids to "eat all your chocolate because there are children without candy in some foreign country that the Hershey's company hasn't discovered yet." Nor have I had to sit patiently while my kids lamented, "Are we having French fries again?!" the way they do about broccoli-chicken casserole. The closest we've come to matching the "food pyramid" is when my son spilled his entire plate and his mashed potatoes landed on the floor in a cone shape.

I think chocolate French fries sound gross, but because I'm a scientific-minded guy, I gave the high-powered food-marketing executives the benefit of the doubt. To confirm their product enhancement decisions, I decided to conduct a dinnertime focus group of the children in our household.

"Tonight, instead of the usual pleasant dinner conversation, I will ask a few questions about your eating habits," I began. "First question. What is your favorite. . . ."

"Dad, what are we having for dessert?" interrupts Maria.

"If we answer all the questions, can we have two desserts?" pleads Paul.

"You forgot to say grace," reminds my wife.

I lead my family in prayer. Sometimes I let my kids lead us in grace, but not tonight. I'm afraid the focus group results would be tainted by prayers such as, "Oh Lord, have mercy on us who are forced to eat vegetables" and "Take pity on us when our parents serve peas." You'd think they'd appreciate the way dinner arrives on the table each night as if it's manna from heaven.

I continue my questioning.

"If you had a choice of eating Brussels sprouts or spinach, which would you pick?"

"Could I put ketchup on them?" asks Maria. She would eat Styrofoam if it were covered in ketchup.

"Nope. No ketchup."

"Don't be gross, Dad," she says, rolling her eyes.

Annie stuffs half a grilled cheese sandwich into her mouth and smiles broadly. I take that to mean she agrees with her older sister.

Next question. "Of the following three things, which is not mandatory at meals: 1) grace, 2) manners, 3) cheese?"

"We don't need cheese if we're eating macaroni and cheese," answers Paul. "It already has cheese in it."

Annie, who is now crawling under the table, discovers a piece of hot dog and pops it into her mouth. I'm taken aback, not because she's eating off the floor but because we haven't eaten hot dogs since last Thursday.

Last question. "What do you think of chocolate French fries?" I ask.

"Ewww! Chocolate French fries!?" they shout in unison. "That's gross! Can we buy some?"

"How do you feel about green ketchup?" I follow up.

"Yuk! That's disgusting! Could we put the green ketchup on the chocolate French fries?"

Maybe those food-marketing executives aren't so crazy after all.

Clearly my kids like gross food. So does my younger brother.

My younger brother once sent me a can of "Mr. Squid" baked cuttlefish chips as a present. He said I probably had trouble finding squid chips in Ohio, being so far from the coast and all. He picked out the Mr. Squid brand because, as it says on the can, they're "spicy, crispy, and fun." (Mr. Squid is a product of Thailand, so don't go looking for Nacho Squid Doritos on your grocer's shelves.)

At first, I had my doubts. I searched the Internet to see if squid chips were a genuine product. (I wouldn't want to be fooled with cheap, imitation cuttlefish.) I quickly found two pieces of information that turned my stomach: 1) Contaminated cuttlefish chips spread food poisoning throughout Japan. 2) Squid chips come up when you search for the phrase "worst chips ever." The advice on one Web site said that squid chips smell much worse than they taste and to hold your nose when you eat them. As a rule, I try to avoid foods that force me to hold my nose.

When my older brother was in college and I was still in high school, I sent him some home cooking. It wasn't brownies—it was meatloaf, mashed potatoes, and gravy poured into a shoebox and mailed fourth class so it could age on the way. Most people define "gag gifts" as items that poke fun at the recipient. I define a gag gift as one that provides the same sensation as having a cotton swab stuck halfway down your throat to see if you have strep. If there's no audible "aacckkkkkkk" sound, it's not a gag gift.

I also adhere to the "teasing is loving" philosophy taught to me by my dad. He practiced what he preached. After a wonderful family dinner, Dad would enthusiastically ask, "Who wants chocolate chip cookies for dessert!?" When my four siblings and I yelled, "We do!" he would respond, "Too bad nobody made any." If that's not love, I don't know what is. My dad's teasing-is-loving philosophy came in especially handy when he asked me what I was mailing to my older brother. I could truthfully answer that I was sending him a big box-o-love—with gravy.

The squid chips, however, were a gift, which brought me to a dilemma—how to write the thank-you note for such a thoughtful present. When my older brother received his "dinner-in-a-box," he showed extremely bad manners by never writing a thank-you note. I didn't want to be accused of the same poor etiquette by my younger brother, so I put pen to paper to thank him for Mr. Squid.

My dearest brother,

Mother taught us the importance of thank-you notes. She etched the three-part format onto our young minds: 1) thank the giver, 2) name the gift, and 3) tell the giver how much you're enjoying the gift. This foolproof format worked well for every present I ever received as a kid—"Thank you, grandma, for the new baseball glove. I played catch with it all afternoon and didn't drop a single throw." Two sentences and my obligation was discharged. But now I've received your present.

Beginning is easy. Thank you for the can of spicy, crispy, and fun Mr. Squid baked cuttlefish chips. There, I've accomplished the first two steps. Please forgive me if I falter on step number three, as words cannot express my enjoyment.

I was waiting until I finished the can of Mr. Squid before writing to thank you, but now I realize that I will never finish it. In fact, I can't force myself to eat a single chip. Like a good father, I made the kids try the chips first. Paul spit his halfway across the room. Maria ran screaming from the house.

I brought the can of Mr. Squid to work and put it next to the doughnuts and coffee. Only one coworker sampled the chips, and she still has the taste in her mouth. That was from three weeks ago. We had to have the office fumigated to remove the squid smell.

Nevertheless, I am confident that my joy from Mr. Squid will reach new heights when you open your birthday present from me next fall. As the saying goes, there is more joy in giving Mr. Squid than in receiving.

Your loving brother.

That was five years ago, and my brother still refuses to open any presents from me.

I once read a magazine article about creative ways to get your kids to eat. Many of the ideas had to do with having your kids help prepare meals. One recipe that stood out called for pieces of bread on which the child painted pictures with a mixture of milk and food coloring. When the child finished painting, the bread was toasted to "dry the paint." The parent then made a sandwich using the work of art, and the child was supposed to eat it.

I don't know if that recipe was kid-tested, but it seems to me that it wouldn't get kids to eat their meal, it would only make preparing lunch take ten times longer. "Painted sandwiches" aren't much different from coloring Easter eggs, which my kids love to do, even though they've never eaten a hard-boiled egg. "Coloring is fun," they say. "Hard-boiled eggs taste yucky."

Eating out at a nice restaurant with your children is a different kind of recipe you might try. It's a "recipe for disaster." Here's how I make it.

Scrub three children thoroughly and place in a minivan. Add two adults. Make sure children cannot touch each other. Drive to a fancy restaurant. Remove children from van. Slide family into restaurant.

When no tables are available, stuff family into a small booth. Garnish children with crayons and crackers to keep them occupied while waiting for menus.

When no menus arrive for twenty minutes, begin to simmer until you stew. When you reach a boil, shout for a waiter.

Do not mince words. Tell waiter you knead service. Toss waiter a few compliments and smother him in kindness until he melts. Layer it on thick.

When your meals never arrive, steep in your kids' fidgeting. When your last bit of patience has been shredded, dissolve into tears. Pare, peel, poach, whip, chop, baste, and dice the menus.

While continuing to boil, remove family from restaurant and roll them into the van. Whip out of parking lot and into fast food drive-thru window. Order family-size bucket of chicken. Beat traffic home.

Serving suggestion: fried chicken with glasses of milk and heaps of sibling bickering on the side.

Hold the bickering, you say? That'd be a miracle.

Daddy's NOT Going to Buy You a Mockingbird, and Other Miraculous Ways to Save Money

I was going on a business trip, so I called in my children and entrusted each of them with my possessions. To my oldest, I gave ten dollars; to my middle child, I gave five dollars; and to my youngest, one dollar—each according to his or her ability. Then I left on my trip.

When I returned, I asked each child what he or she had done with the money.

My oldest came forward with the ten dollars and an additional ten. She said, "Father, you gave me ten dollars. See, I have made ten more."

"Well done, my good child," I said. "How did you accomplish this?"

"I took five from my younger brother and rifled through Mom's purse for the other five," she said.

"Since you were resourceful in small matters, I will give you greater responsibilities," I said. "Go clean your room and then take out the trash. By the way, you're grounded."

Then my middle child, who had received five dollars, came forward. "Father, you gave me five dollars. See, I now have ten."

"I thought your sister took your five," I asked. "How did you get ten?"

"I am also resourceful," he said. "I visited Grandma and Grandpa and convinced them to pay me two dollars to be quiet. Then I sold your lawn mower for eight dollars."

"Well done, my good child," I said. "Since you were resourceful in small matters, I will give you greater responsibilities. Pick up your toys and sweep the kitchen floor. By the way, no television for a month."

Then my youngest child, who had received one dollar, came forward. "Da-da," she said, because she couldn't talk yet.

"Where is the dollar I gave you?" I asked.

She pointed to the backyard. We went out and dug in the mulch wherever she pointed but found nothing.

"Why did you bury your dollar?" I asked her. "Did you think I was a demanding father, harvesting where I did not plant and gathering where I did not scatter, so out of fear you buried your dollar in the ground?"

She laughed. "Da-da," she said again. (I'm not very effective at instilling fear in my children.) We couldn't find the dollar, so went back inside where the other two kids were doing their chores.

"Why doesn't she have to do chores like us?" the two older children asked.

"She's not as resourceful as you," I replied.

Then there was wailing and gnashing of teeth—but that part is typical at our house.

Money and children are an interesting combination. A groundbreaking study commissioned by the Center for a New American Dream discovered something parents would have never guessed: Children nag their parents to buy them things.

According to the national survey, children age twelve to seventeen ask an average nine times for things they want until their parents finally give in. My kids average a whopping twenty-two nags before I buckle. I've always said my kids are above average—now's there's proof. (Note: The national study had a margin of error of plus or minus three nags. My kids have never been minus a nag.)

"Amazingly, more than ten percent of twelve- to thirteen-year-olds admit to asking their parents more than fifty times for products they've seen advertised," the Center's study reads. I don't doubt the veracity of that finding. Paul once nagged me 171 times in a single breath for some food product with Bob the Builder on the box. (Can we drive Dad crazy? Yes we can!)

The financial findings are what really surprised me. The study said kids spent a record $155 billion of their own money in a single year. That's some allowance. Summer jobs must pay a lot more today than when I was a kid. No wonder the lemonade stand down the street charges $123,000 a glass. The warm six-ounce plastic cup is almost as expensive as a Grande Latte at Starbucks.

The five-year-old proprietor told me he's franchising his "Lemonade Hut" concept and asked me if I "wanted in at the ground floor."

You'd think kids would be satisfied with their own billions, but James McNeal, kids marketing expert, says children exert enough pressure to influence more than $500 billion of their parents' purchases per year. Either there are a lot of successful, young negotiators out there, or one kid talked his parents into buying him some very expensive stuff—like the Space Shuttle or a pair of designer sneakers. My kids influenced $19.95 of my purchases last year. I bought a case of bungee cords to keep them in their beds at night—a very prudent investment.

The Center for a New American Dream provides some tips for decreasing the nag factor. They suggest parents establish limits on TV watching and keep the TV in a public area of the house. I disagree. Unlimited TV watching and keeping the set in a private part of the house have worked for our family and can work for yours too. The private part of the house is the closet. Before placing the TV in the closet, set it to The Weather Channel, and remove the channel button. Wait until your kids go in, slam the door shut, and lock it.

The Center also suggests that parents make dinnertime special. Try to have a meal together with the whole family—even if it's only once or twice a week. I recommend a table for two right outside the closet where the kids are watching the seven-day forecast. Purchase Pop-Tarts, cheese slices, and other flat foods that slide easily under the door.

A nice, quiet meal with the whole family. Now that's a New American Dream I can get excited about.

I think the real problem with kids' monetary expectations is rooted in the lullabies we sing to them. I've sung every imaginable lullaby to my kids. Some lullabies I've known for my entire life but have never stopped to think about the words—until recently. Now I believe "Hush Little Baby" should be banned because it gives children a warped sense of consumer responsibility as well as false expectations about what they might be receiving as gifts.

"Hush Little Baby" would be more aptly named "The Defective Product" song. The bird doesn't sing, the ring turns to brass, and the looking glass breaks, among other problems. I'm sure none of these products is under warranty any longer, either. And the icing on the cake is that the song tells children "not to say a word" about the defective items. I suspect the song was written by a consortium of Communist novelty manufacturers who didn't want kids complaining about broken toys.

In addition to sending kids the wrong message about consumer advocacy, "Hush Little Baby" provides gift ideas that have no place being in my kids' heads.

Daddy's NOT going to buy you a mockingbird. My kids mock each other enough as it is. They don't need a bird to teach them any new tricks. I can just hear that mockingbird singing, "You're having a time-oooooout and I'mmmmmmmm nooooooooot." No thank you.

Daddy's NOT going to buy you a diamond ring. There will be no purchases of expensive jewelry for my children. Maria has a game called "Pretty, Pretty Princess." It contains mounds of costume jewelry. The object of the game is to get all your color jewelry pieces, as well as the silver crown. Then, you're the pretty, pretty princess! Paul has a different version of the game: See which pieces of jewelry fit into the heating registers, then hide the remaining pieces in every corner of the house. The winner is the one who drives his sister crazy. Before we lost all the pieces, Paul and I actually played the game. He won. I'm saving the photos of him dressed as the pretty, pretty princess to share with his prom date.

Daddy's NOT going to buy you a looking glass. I don't like to buy presents that might break. Unfortunately, that includes any gift I might consider buying my kids. They are masters of destruction. If there is only one toy in the middle of the living room floor, Paul feels compelled to stand on it as if he would fall into molten lava if he set foot on the carpet. One of my young nephews once said, while opening a birthday present, "This is going to be really hard to break." He didn't mean that the toy car was durable. He meant that he would have to use extraordinary measures to demolish it. If I gave my kids a brick for a present, it might last forty-eight hours. A looking glass wouldn't last two minutes.

Daddy's NOT going to buy you a billy goat. As you know, I have 672 rules for my children. Rule #347 is "No goats in the house."

Daddy's NOT going to buy you a cart and mule. If I were inclined to purchase a cart and mule, which I am not, I would first read the crash test results in *Consumer Reports* magazine. Apparently the cart and mule's axle length wasn't sufficient to keep it from turning over. This model cart and mule will no doubt be recalled by General Motors any day now.

Daddy's NOT going to buy you a dog named Rover. One question: If you had a dog named Rover who wouldn't bark, wouldn't you consider yourself lucky? Besides my neighbor, whose dogs bark incessantly, I don't know of anyone who thinks nonstop yapping is a positive trait for a pet.

Daddy's NOT going to buy you a horse and cart. Why would I buy my kids a horse and cart after the cart and mule fiasco? Certainly, I would have learned my lesson. I might purchase the Western Barbie equestrian set with genuine cowgirl outfit (including lariat) and faithful steed Cinnamon. But, before I actually gave the present to my daughter, I would superglue Barbie's boots to her feet so they wouldn't join the other pairs of tiny plastic stiletto heels in our vacuum cleaner.

Don't get me started on "Rock-a-Bye Baby." I've checked the Consumer Product Safety Commission's Web site, and cradles are not intended to be mounted in treetops.

Even without the presents suggested in "Hush Little Baby," raising children can be expensive. But there are also many ways having a large family can save you thousands of dollars.

If you have only one child, you're bound to spoil him or her rotten. This can be expensive. Many first-time parents have no idea that it is cheaper to buy an actual Amtrak train than the complete 62,000-piece Thomas the Tank Engine toy train set. If you have only one child, it's wise to buy stock in several major toy companies just to offset your toy expenditures.

Even so, your child will have the uncanny ability to sit in a room surrounded by playthings and whine, "Daaaaaaaaaaaaad, I have nothing to plaaaaaay with." This will usually occur just after you've purchased the Deluxe Lego set with which a full-size, four-bedroom ranch can be constructed.

The solution, of course, is more kids. There is nothing that makes a child more interested in a toy than a sibling who is playing with it. I have watched my kids ignore newly opened birthday presents to fight over an old drinking straw. In emergencies, simply tell your children that they may not play with the leaves in the yard and— botta bing, botta boom—they will race outside and happily fight over them for hours.

Don't buy a surround-sound system for your television—have more kids! Two children provide stereo sound. Five will create a complete surround-sound system that will ensure noise is all around you . . . always. (Volume control not included.) Traditional surround-sound systems sit in your family room. Your kids will follow you wherever you go. This wireless version is much more state-of-the-art and will be the envy of all your friends.

Need an Internet-ready refrigerator with a computer embedded in the door that keeps track of which food items you've used and automatically reorders them? (Yes, this product actually exists.) Of course you don't need one—at least not when you have lots of children. Your kids will keep constant tabs on what is in your refrigerator by standing in front of the fridge for hours with the door wide open. They'll also provide a warning signal that can be heard for two blocks when important food items are running low. ("Mom! We're out of milk!")

Reading the covers of decorating magazines while in the grocery check-out line can make you realize how inadequate your home is. Not just inadequate—pitifully lackluster and perhaps tasteless. The magazines scream, "White walls? Shame on you!" What you need . . . want . . . must have . . . is a faux-finished, sponge-painted, crackle look with a country-French border. This is the same look that you'll get if you serve your children a lunch consisting entirely of condiments, substitute paint brushes for forks and spoons, and leave the house for an hour. (The crackle finish will appear after the mustard dries.) While two children can finish an average size kitchen in a single meal, six can do the entire house. Think of the savings over hiring an expensive interior decorator. It's not just ketchup on your walls, it's money in your pocket. Which brings me to distressed furniture.

It seems some people will pay significantly more for a new table that has been banged with chains, nicked up, and rubbed with dirt. Instant antiques. Am I missing something here, or can kids make anything in your house look like an antique in less than a nano-second? They can even make the outside of your house look like an antique. You might think our family's house was built circa 1900. Actually, we built it a few years ago. Now I'm distressed, too.

So, don't run to your personal computer to calculate the monumental cost of additional offspring. Calculate the huge savings you'll accrue by having four, eight, or even ten kids! You might even become a millionaire. (A friend of mine growing up had eleven siblings. I think his dad became independently wealthy from his distressed furniture business.)

But the real bottom line is more children equals more love in your house. And that's worth more than anything money can buy.

My Wife Has Miraculous Superpowers

On the planet Smellefra, my wife would be revered as a superheroine with miraculous powers. Here's how I figure it. Superman came from the planet Krypton. On Earth, he has superhuman strength, x-ray vision, supersensitive hearing, and a host of other miraculous abilities. But on Krypton, everyone had those abilities, so Superman was quite ordinary. Every kid on the playgrounds of Krypton could change the planet's orbit with his or her superbreath. Big deal.

Once I had this brainstorm, I realized that every member of my family possesses superpowers—abilities that appear normal at first glance but would make us superheroes on other planets. We may even be from another planet. Our neighbors have thought so for years.

Listen to this. While visiting a farm, my wife used her miraculous supersniffing power to distinguish between two unpleasant odors that would make mere mortals' eyes water. While strolling across the barnyard, inhabited by cows, goats, and pigs, she turned to me and said, "I think Annie needs a new diaper."

"Egads!" I shouted. "You're able to detect a dirty diaper in the midst of a barnyard that smells, well, like a barnyard! Where were you born, woman, the planet Smellefra?!"

Of course, I was joking when I mentioned the planet Smellefra. Everyone knows that Smellotopians have no noses. My wife would be revered as a superheroine had she been born there. There may even be a Smellefrian comic book that chronicles my wife's supernasal ability. When a ten-year-old Smellotopian girl is kidnapped by terrorists from the planet Stinkarius, who do they call on to track down the smell of the culprits? My wife, of course.

Superman has the ability to hear a pin drop from one hundred miles away. My children, on the other hand, have the miraculous ability to ignore commands from their parents, who are only a few feet away. That explains those hearing test results. My kids must use some sound-wave jamming technique, probably learned on their home planet, to nullify undesirable requests that might penetrate their eardrums and cause them to exert strenuous effort, such as coming to the dinner table. The fascinating thing is their ability to discern between different sounds at the same instant. To test their powers, I have asked them to pick up their toys while at the same time an ice cream truck was playing its jingle in the State of New Mexico. We live in Ohio. Using their miraculous power, my kids were able to hear the truck but ignore my voice.

It would be nice to live in Superman's Fortress of Solitude so I could rest and think without interruption.

Unfortunately, my kids have not stopped talking since the day they were born and have the miraculous ability to continue talking even when no one is listening. (Either that or Maria is able to converse with our refrigerator and I just can't detect the fridge's response because it's at a frequency that only dogs and young girls can hear.)

Like Superman, I also have superpowered eyes. Superman has the ability to see right through solid walls. I have the ability to look right past a full wastebasket without even noticing that it needs to be taken out.

But my wife has the miraculous ability to see right through me.

While mothers and wives have many miraculous powers, it is a good thing they don't see their job description before they accept the position. Even with miraculous powers, it's tough duty.

My job, on the other hand, is easy. I get to write a lot and work with friendly, talented people. I like my job even more since Maria started studying occupations at school. Seeing my wife's and my occupation through my daughter's eyes was revealing.

Maria's assignment was to draw a picture of her parents' jobs. Her drawing of me showed a man sitting a desk, typing quietly at a computer while drinking a cup of coffee. Very nice. Maria's drawing of my wife was not as pleasant. The picture showed Mom standing in front of the sink washing dishes while Paul was hitting a crying Annie. Mom has her arms raised above her head and is screaming, "I can't take it anymore!" That Kodak moment isn't going to attract too many job applicants.

At least Maria didn't write the job descriptions to go with our occupations. Even fast food restaurants sugarcoat their job description: Be part of a team! Free uniforms! Complimentary meals! My wife's job description would tell the real story.

Help wanted: Mother

> **Seven-day workweek with twenty-four-hour shifts. Some vacation time accrues after first eighteen years. Must be able to cook at least ten dishes none of the kids will eat. Ability to tune out crying a must. Should be able to carry infant and three bags of groceries at same time. Must have chauffeur's license and advanced degrees in nursing, veterinary medicine, and education while not too proud to be a seamstress and maid. Must be able to juggle schedules while balancing a checkbook as well as be willing to be spit-up upon. Requires willingness to change dirty diapers, flat tires, and plans at the last minute. No previous experience necessary because no previous experience can prepare you for this job. Children willing to break in new recruits.**

Being broken in by your children is a hard way to learn. It would be convenient if a parent boot camp existed. Before their first child was born, moms- and dads-to-be could enlist as "parent recruits" and have a demanding drill instructor run them through a gauntlet of exercises to toughen them up. Boot camp would include physical and mental tests and challenges. It would show the recruits what they were made of and increase their confidence. It would also give them a taste of what they would soon endure as parents.

It would be difficult to get actual children to cooperate with the boot camp exercises. Kids value the element of surprise and wouldn't want to give any parent the upper hand. So, the drill instructors would have to develop tasks to simulate the experience of taking care of children.

On the first day of boot camp, the recruits would roll out of bed at 5 a.m. and dress for a ten-mile hike. Ten miles is the average distance a parent runs around in the morning to help the kids find their clothes and collect school things before sending them out the door. Each recruit would start the hike with an empty knapsack and fill it with books, permission slips, and lunch money found along the way, until it reaches seventy-five pounds.

Once back from the hike, the parents would jog to the infant feeding range for target practice. The range consists of a row of electric fans with thimbles attached to the blades. When a recruit is positioned in front of the fan, the drill instructor would turn the fan to high and give the recruit a spoon and a jar of pureed vegetable medley baby food. The recruit would then attempt to fill the rapidly spinning thimbles with the baby food, which is slightly easier than feeding a live infant.

After heading to the showers to remove the baby food mixed with sweat from the hike, the recruits would run—

double time—to the shopping simulation installation. Using a standard-issue shopping cart, each recruit would be responsible for collecting 150 items from the grocery store shelves—using coupons to get the best deals—while also herding a group of twenty cats. Herding cats is the closest thing to trying to keep your children with you at the supermarket. To make the simulation a little more realistic, the cats will not have been fed that day and will attempt to eat things off the shelves. Any recruit failing to complete the shopping simulation in the allotted time is required to do fifty one-handed pushups, while using the other hand to pick toys up off the floor.

After a lunch eaten on top of a washing machine while folding towels, the recruits are given high altitude training. As the drill instructor hits one ball after another onto the roof of a house, the recruits must hoist a ladder to the edge, climb it, and remove the balls from the rain gutter.

Next there's the traditional boot camp-type obstacle course—except that this one is in the dark, providing extensive training for getting to kids having bad dreams in the middle of the night. The obstacle course has to be negotiated at the same time the recruit is negotiating a higher allowance with a teenager. The teenager is played by a portable CD player with a recording that repeats "But my friends get bigger allowances" over and over and over.

Finally, at the end of the day, it's time for the war game simulation, in which the recruits infiltrate enemy territory and rescue two POWs from school. They must use defensive driving techniques to penetrate the hostile territory of a school parking lot crammed with parents trying to be the first to find their kids and get home. Recruits are encouraged to bribe crossing guards and use other forms of military intelligence.

On second thought, maybe it's better that parents aren't trained before their children are born. Sometimes, ignorance is bliss.

My wife's job description also includes "gardener." And she has the miraculous ability to get me to do crazy things—like audition plants.

You have to watch your wife every minute or the next thing you know, she'll be purchasing subversive materials. Of course, I'm referring to gardening books. I paid no attention to a recent hardcover acquisition made by my wife until we were planting some new flowers in front of our house. She had hurt her arm and I was helping her with a few new additions to her garden. As I was patting down the soil around the first plant, she said, "We'll audition that plant there for a while."

"Audition?" I had heard of people talking to their plants but never asking their plants to talk back. I don't know much about gardening, so I went along for the ride. I seem to do a lot of that. Since the plant was Russian Sage, I used my best Russian accent and moved the leaves of the plant with my hands as I made the plant speak.

"My Englesh not berry gut," I ventriloquized for the plant, "but I wut like to be in your beautiful garden, berry, berry much."

"Not that type of audition," said my wife. "*Audition* means that we don't know if that's the exact spot we want the plant to be planted in."

"We" was a terribly strong word to use. I knew that this was exactly the spot I wanted the plant to be. Its roots were covered. It was at that moment I first realized I was morally opposed to transplanting anything. Then I had the sudden realization that we had dozens of plants left to audition. I felt a great desire to rearrange furniture.

"Wouldn't our couch look much better against the other wall in the living room?" I hinted. My wife wouldn't take the bait and asked me to replant the sage three inches to the left.

I like my concept of plant auditions much better than my wife's. I was ready for the Hollyhocks to audition as Buddy Hollyhocks and sing, "That will be the day, that I'm fertilized." The White Nancy Spotted Dead Needle became White Nancy Sinatra in my mind and sang, "These roots were made for walking." The Sunny Bono Blue Speedwell chimed in with, "I've got you, bulb." The May West Sage coaxed, "Come up and seed me some time." All the Lily Tomlin of the Valley could say was, "Is this the pear tree to whom I am speaking?"

The Johnny Jumpup would have done a great monologue as Johnny Carson Jumpup.

"Tim is such a dumb gardener . . ." he would have begun, pausing while the other plants yelled, "How dumb is he!?" "Tim is so dumb, he wouldn't plant any bellflower because he was afraid the neighbors would complain about the noise."

I stopped the auditions immediately. When I start to insult myself through the mouth of a plant, it's time to call it quits.

When I first saw the plant book that taught my wife the auditioning concept, it looked harmless enough. (In an effort to protect other husbands, I won't mention the book's title.) The tagline on the cover read, "The 150 Best Perennials for Great-Looking, Trouble-Free Gardens." Great-looking, yes. Trouble-free, no.

What shocked me most were the words I found in the first few pages of the book.

"Don't be shy about digging up and moving plants that don't look right. . . . It's tough to get the garden right the first time, and half the fun is in the tweaking that follows."

If digging up plants and moving them is half the fun, the other half must be stepping on the tines of a rake and feeling the handle smack you square in the face.

Perhaps I overreacted to my wife's request to move the sage. My behavior may have been caused by a traumatic experience I had a few summers ago when I received a call from my brother-in-law. He needed help moving something, so I gladly drove over to his house. I expected an old refrigerator or some other large appliance to be waiting. Instead, the object was an eight-foot tall tree that he wanted to dig up and move six inches to the right because it lined up with the lamppost in his front yard. That's a true story that proves one thing: My wife didn't buy the book after all. She borrowed it from her brother.

It's a good thing my wife has all her miraculous superpowers, because there's no tougher job than being a mother. The next time Maria gets an assignment to draw a picture of her mom's occupation, I hope she gets all the details correct. In her original drawing Maria forgot to draw in the halo above her mom's head.

In the Beginning There Was No Duct Tape, and Other Miraculous Do-It-Yourself Projects

God created the world before Home Depot existed. That's a theological concept I can't comprehend. I take at least five trips to Home Depot during every project. The first trip is to buy materials, the second is to return what I purchased and get the correct items, the third is to ask questions, the fourth is because I forgot the answers, and the fifth to ask if I can pay someone to do the project for me.

Obviously, God is a better creator than I am. God created the entire universe. I can barely assemble a gas grill. Frankly, I have never completed a project and said, "It is good."

There are thousands of ways my ability to create pales in comparison to God's. For example, during the creation of the world, God separated the light from the darkness. I've separated an egg, and my children when they fight, but that's about it. God called the light Day, and the darkness he called Night. I called my neighbor to borrow a metric wrench to assemble the grill.

If I had created the world, my first words would have been, "Let there be duct tape to keep the stars from falling out of the sky and to hold the leaves on the trees." Not God. His project was free of artificial adhesives. In my opinion, that's more miraculous than creating man from dust. God didn't even use a coat hanger—the universal household tool. Amazing!

Not once during the six days did God have to go back and fix what he messed up the previous day. That raises the theological question: Did God have instructions when creating the world? Some scripture scholars believe God had instructions but didn't read them, proving God is a man. Other scholars argue that God cannot be a man because there were no leftover parts on the sixth day when the project was completed. I'm no Bible expert, but if God were a man, I doubt he would have started the project in the first place. God created the world "in the beginning." Men never start a project in the beginning but rather wait for their wives—or mothers—to ask four or five times.

I have discovered two ways I resemble the Creator. First, it takes me the same amount of time to assemble a gas grill as it took God to create the world: six days. Second, God rested on the seventh day. My wife says when it comes to napping, not even God is better than I am.

Now, Noah was a man who knew how to assemble things. I might attempt to build a small deck attached to my house, but I doubt I'd try to build a houseboat with three decks, like Noah. Even if I did, my wife wouldn't trust it to float.

When I read the story of Noah in the Bible, I can't help thinking that the directions to build the ark left out a few steps. In Genesis, Noah is instructed to follow five steps.

Step 1: **Make yourself an ark of gopher wood (length: 300 cubits; width: 50 cubits; height: 30 cubits).**

Step 2: **Put various compartments in the ark with a bottom, second, and third deck.**

Step 3: **Make an opening for daylight.**

Step 4: **Put a door in the side.**

Step 5: **Cover the ark with pitch, inside and out.**

Is it just me, or is this like asking someone to build an airplane by instructing him to "make a fuselage, attach wings, put in windows, and insert an engine"?

Because Noah's instructions were so sparse—and I doubt Noah had previous ark-building experience—I can come to only one conclusion. Noah watched Home & Garden Television (HGTV).

I'm sure HGTV didn't have the exact same programs back then. The shows probably focused more on tent and pyramid building and renovation. You know, shows like "Awesome Tent Interiors" and "Dream Pyramid." There must also have been a program called "This Old Ark" that helped Noah get the job done. Let's listen in on the show with its hosts, Gomer and Meshech. . . .

Gomer: **Don't you just hate it when you were planning to go to Disney World, God announces the end of the world, and you have to build an ark on short notice?**

Meshech: **Not any old ark, an ark that's 300 cubits long and 50 cubits wide—now that's a project.**

Gomer: **Today we'll show you some ark-building tricks and tips so you can get that ark built and still make it to Disney World. You won't even have to fly since you'll have your own transportation after you're finished, ha, ha.**

Meshech: **Very funny. Just make sure the hotel you plan to stay in allows pets because you'll be coming with a boatload of 'em.**

Gomer: **So, to start we went to Ark Depot to buy our gopher wood. Art Depot is this show's sponsor and the place for all your boating projects.**

Meshech: **What is gopher wood, anyway?**

Gomer: **Gopher wood is when God tells you to build an ark and you "go-for" wood. Ha, ha, I've got a million of 'em.**

Meshech: **I know. I just wish you'd keep them to yourself. So, while we were at Ark Depot, we** picked up a book of ark plans, since God didn't specify the model he wanted. We chose the Catalina, which sleeps twenty people and 6,000 animals. Just what the boss ordered.

Gomer: Now, because nails haven't been invented yet, we're going to assemble our gopher wood using wooden pegs. We showed our plans to a craftsman at Ark Depot, and he cut our gopher wood into the size pieces our plan calls for.

Meshech: Very convenient, especially since it looks like I see some storm clouds over there.

Gomer: Now that we've got the ark together, we just punch out the pre-perforated windows and door and we're set to sail.

Meshech: Well, that wasn't as difficult as I thought it would be.

Gomer: Building projects are never difficult when you can stop the camera and have a team of real carpenters come in to do the work.

Meshech: That's a great trick for our viewers at home to remember. When your wife leaves in the morning, call a carpenter to finish your project and then take credit for doing the work when she returns. Nudge, nudge, wink, wink.

Gomer: Now you're using your head, Meshech.

Meshech: **We'll see you next time when we'll show you how to build your very own Tower of Babel.**

Gomer: **We never seem to be able to finish that project. . . .**

Shortly after *This Old Ark* ended, "the fountains of the great deep burst forth, and the windows of the heavens were opened," which sounds remarkably similar to what happened when I tried to fix a leaky pipe in our basement.

My ineptitude with mechanical tasks isn't something new. I trace its roots to my junior high school wood shop class, which instilled in me a fear of mechanical devices. That's why I had to call my life insurance company last summer when my lawn needed mowing.

"Can you send someone over to cut my grass?" I asked.

"We're a life insurance company, not a lawn service," replied the representative.

"I'm well aware of that," I said, a tad miffed. "My life insurance policy is with you. I just had my lawnmower blade sharpened and reattached it to the mower myself. I figure it's cheaper for you to pay someone to cut my lawn than have the blade slip off my mower and cause you the inconvenience of mailing a large check to my mourning wife."

"I still don't understand," said the puzzled representative.

"You obviously haven't looked in my insurance file to see who my seventh grade industrial arts instructor was," I said. "Let me fill you in."

Like all the other kids in my class, I was looking forward to taking wood shop in junior high school. But my mind quickly changed.

I can't remember our teacher's name, but Dr. Death comes to mind. He bore no resemblance to the friendly craftsmen on *This Old House*, although he was safety conscious in a strange sort of way. The first thing he did was provide a tour of the woodworking machinery.

"This is the band saw," said Dr. Death. "See my fingers? Cut off three of 'em, zip, zip, zip, just like butter. Let that be a lesson to you."

His fingers had been reattached, but I made a mental note to never set foot near the band saw. Next on the tour was the buffer.

"Once a student was wearing a tie when he used this buffer," said Dr. Death. "Tie got caught and dragged his entire body in, starting with his head. All that was left was his right foot. Let that be a lesson to you."

I added the buffer to the list of tools I refused to use. A list that continued to grow as we were shown the belt sander, jigsaw, and drill press.

Students were required sign up for each machine they wanted to use. Dr. Death said it was to keep order in the classroom. I'm sure it was to notify next of kin. Even the hand tools were regulated. Each of us had three metal circles into which were punched our ID number. We had to provide one circle for each tool we needed. That would narrow down the police work when trying to determine the cause of death. Each time I reluctantly checked out a hand tool, I said a prayer that my mother wouldn't receive a phone call from the coroner's office.

"Looks like your son succumbed to a piece of 100-grit sandpaper," I imagined the coroner telling my mother. "Either that or a small Phillips-head screwdriver."

When we began work on our birdfeeders, some students threw caution to the wind and used the high-powered death tools. I opted for a safer route.

"Why were you late today?" asked Dr. Death.

"I had to check my shirt for loose threads so the buffer wouldn't suck me in from across the room," I said.

He laughed. It was a maniacal laugh, but I was glad I amused him.

"What are you using to cut that board?" he asked.

"A pair of fingernail clippers," I replied.

"That will never work!" he shouted, aghast.

"Perhaps not, but at least I'll live to tell about it."

"That reminds me," said Dr. Death, "did I ever tell you about the student who tried to trim his fingernails using the pneumatic drill press?" Before I could answer he asked another question.

"What's that you're sanding with?"

"A piece of the softest felt I could find," I replied.

"The birds in your yard will starve before you finish your feeder using those tools," he said, obviously disgusted.

"I've watched Alfred Hitchcock's movie *The Birds*," I said. "I think my odds are better with them than the band saw."

It was a minor miracle that I survived the class. After my experience, I decided to drop the electrical shop class I was registered for. While I could avoid power tools for the rest of my life, avoiding electrical outlets would prove a bit more difficult.

"So, you see," I finished telling the insurance representative, "when you think about it, a lawn mower is no more than a combination band saw and buffer. I've just reattached my freshly sharpened lawnmower blade, and I'm sure death and destruction will ensue if I actually use it."

There was silence on the telephone line for about a minute. Then the voice asked, "Have you considered cutting your grass using your fingernail clippers?"

Just goes to show you should never call your insurance company to get your grass cut. I guess I should have had someone at Home Depot reattach my lawnmower blade in the first place.

A Perfect Child—The Miracle of Christmas

My wife realizes I'm not the handiest person around the house. That's because *she's* the handiest. I lied when I said it took me six days to put together our gas grill. It took me five days and twenty-three hours of frustration before I finally asked my wife for help. She's an engineer.

My ineptitude really shines forth on Christmas Eve when I have to assemble presents for our kids. Here's a glimpse into our house.

'Twas the night before Christmas, when all through the house,
Not a creature was stirring, not even my spouse;
With only six hours left, until morning light,
Assembling kids' presents would take me all night.

19,000 pieces—bolts, washers, and screws,
To be put together, and me with no clue;

All I had for tools were some needle-nose pliers,
A Swiss Army knife and a Phillips screwdriver.

When out on the lawn there arose such a racket,
I threw down my pliers and put on my jacket;
I swung open the door, to check out the noise,
And saw a red-suited man, bringing more toys.

I shouted, "Hey, you on my lawn, what's the idea?"
As my shrubs were being eaten by eight small reindeer;
The big man looked up at me and said with a smile,
"There's more to assemble—it will take you awhile."

"My kids don't need more toys," I countered right quick,
But he wouldn't hear "no," that stubborn Saint Nick;
"These new toys have detailed instructions," he said,

And he winked as he lifted a bag from his sled.

Then he pulled a bunch of woodchips out of his bag,
"It's a dollhouse," he said, as he looked at the tag;
"It has 6,000 small pieces, plus one or two,
You can make it if you have a gallon of glue."

"And, there are no axle holes on this toy car,
With only two wheels it won't go very far;
Perhaps you can whip up some rubber for tires,
I'm sure you can do it before you retire."

"But Nick," I pleaded, "don't you have simple toys?
Can't they build simple things—those elves you employ?
How 'bout a ball, a rag doll, or gun that shoots darts,
Or some other present made of only one part?"

Santa said, "Those kinds of toys are passé these days,
It's complicated gadgets that are all the craze;
So, please take these here toys and I'll be on my way,
I have houses to get to and visits to pay."

"I don't want any more toys!" I yelled quite in shock,
Then I slammed the door shut and I secured the lock;
And I took off my coat and went back to my bench,
And tried to read the directions—printed in French.

Then just as I found I was missing a screw,
That old coot came sneaking right down through my flue;
"You forgot all these toys," said the man dressed in red,
Then he put his sack right down and here's what he said.

"You're not alone staying up all through the night,

Dads all over the world are in the same plight;
They don't have the right tools, or any instructions,
Their eyes are bleary and their minds don't quite function."

Then he left me there speechless, alone with my work,
And filled all the stockings, then turned with a jerk;
And laying his finger aside of his nose,
And giving a nod, up the chimney he rose.

He sprang to his sleigh, to his team gave a whistle,
And away they all flew like the down of a thistle;
But I heard him exclaim, as he jumped in his sleigh,
"You'll need 62 batteries—all triple A."

While running out to the QuickMart at midnight to buy batteries is quite a thrill, the thing I like best about Christmas is the holy family. There's Joseph, the devoted father, taking care of his wife and infant son. Mary, the loving mother, holding her new baby close. And, of course, there's Jesus, the perfect child. Paintings of the holy family always make the three appear so peaceful. So serene. So unlike our family around Christmas.

Maria and Paul have a nativity set they love to play with. Each December they carefully place each plastic figurine in the Christmas Eve scenario. Mary and Joseph rest quietly as they gaze upon baby Jesus, asleep in the manger. A donkey and a few sheep graze nearby. The three wise men peer into the crèche, careful not to disturb the peaceful family inside. Behind the wise men, shepherds wait patiently for their turn to look upon the newborn king.

Without warning, a bright red fire engine—guided by Paul's hand—speeds by, knocking over a camel and one of the wise men. Luckily, the frankincense he carries remains securely stuck to his hands and doesn't spill. Princess Barbie, who towers over the others in the nativity scene, narrowly avoids the passing vehicle and stoops low in an attempt to see the babe in the manger. She pushes aside a bright yellow rubber duck and stuffed Dalmatian who block her view. The duck and one of the sheep climb to the roof of the stable and jump onto Thomas the Tank Engine as he steams up and drops off a group of characters from Blues Clues.

Like other kids, Maria and Paul seamlessly blend their toys with their stories. It doesn't bother them a bit that Barbie is the sixty-foot-tall woman compared to the shepherds. While some members of the nativity set are manhandled during play, baby Jesus is pampered. Maria and Paul pretend to change his diaper. Jesus is fed whatever they can whip up in their play kitchen—corn-on-the-cob and cake; cheeseburgers and chicken. He is serenaded with songs—sometimes Christmas carols, other times favorites like the "Hokey Pokey."

Maria and Paul help the wise men decide what types of gifts to bring to baby Jesus. With the myriad choices available today, there's no need to settle for gold, frankincense, and myrrh. Maria and Paul ask me for gift ideas. "Something expensive," they suggest.

I put on my thinking cap. Instead of pondering, "What would Jesus do?" (WWJD), I consider "What should the wise men bring?" (WSTWMB).

"The wise men were rich, intelligent men who gave extravagant presents," I tell Maria and Paul. "So, there's really only one place to look for gifts." We search our recycling bin for a copy of the Sharper Image catalogue.

Our mailbox is jammed with product propaganda during the months before Christmas, which makes me an international expert on specialty catalogues. Notice the fancy spelling: *catalogue*—from the Greek, *catalo*, "to buy," and *gue*, "you don't really want any of these overpriced products but we will convince you that you can't live without them."

"The wise men were astrologers and studied the stars," I explain, "so they would probably love to give some of the latest high-tech gadgets."

Maria and Paul leave the nativity set and jump on the couch next to me.

"How about the Ionic Breeze Quadra Silent Air Purifier," I suggest. "It's a whopping $350. It neutralizes household odors and complies with U.S. safety standards for low ozone emissions."

"Will it work in a stable?" Paul asks.

"Excellent point," I say. "They probably don't have an extension cord long enough to run all the way from the inn to the stable. Besides, it says it works on household odors—not barnyard odor. Perhaps your wise men should consider the Official USAF Stealth Pilot Watch. At a paltry $399, this fine timepiece offers many innovative features, including an extender so you can wear it over a flight suit."

"Jesus was wrapped in swaddling clothes, not a flight suit," Maria points out.

"Very observant," I say. "But, look at this. The watch incorporates an exclusive self-illuminating tritium gas dial, with hands and hour markers that glow brightly for up to twenty-five years, even in absolute blackness. . . ."

"I don't think Jesus likes to be in the dark," says Paul, who is speaking from his own personal experience of dark rooms.

"Okay, maybe the Stealth Watch isn't the best gift for the wise men to give. How about this—a clock that is permanently linked via radio signal to the Official U.S. Atomic Clock in Boulder, Colorado. This atomic clock automatically resets itself each night and is accurate to ten-billionths of a second per day. Wow! If I had that, I'd never be more than 125-millionths of a second late for an appointment again. It comes in a wall mounted version as well as a $699 solar-powered wristwatch." (I point out that the sun and other fiery planets are sold separately.)

"Why would Jesus need to know the time in Boulder, Colorado?" asks Maria. "He's a baby. What could he be late for? You keep suggesting gifts you'd like to get—not ones Jesus would like."

I had a childhood friend who had that gift-giving strategy down to an art. In three consecutive Christmases, he bought his mother a Bobby Hull puzzle, a baseball glove, and a dartboard. Each time, when she looked stumped and politely inquired what she would do with such a gift, he suggested, "Why don't you let me use it?" Clever kid. I think he's a U. S. Senator now.

"You're right," I conceded. "Perhaps I was thinking more about me than Jesus."

I check one last potential present in the catalogue.

"Here's the perfect gift," I say. "The $1,495, deluxe, commercial-quality popcorn popper makes popcorn 'unrivaled by microwaves or hot-air poppers.'"

Unrivaled by about $1,475, I would say. The product did have one redeeming quality. It can make six quarts of popcorn every three minutes. I do the math for Maria and Paul.

"With this popper, you can make 6,570,000 gallons of popcorn when you and your Stealth Pilot Watch are stranded in absolute blackness for twenty-five years," I say.

Maria and Paul like the idea of the wise men bringing a popcorn popper and go back to their game.

"Where's King Herod?" Paul asks, pushing the story along. When I tell him the nativity set didn't come with a King Herod figure, he abducts one of the shepherds and forces him to play the role. Maria quickly grabs an angel and chases Herod away. Herod hotwires a Tonka dump truck and escapes.

With Herod gone, things quiet down. Mary tells Joseph to watch the baby while she goes to the supermarket (located under the ottoman). With groceries in hand, Jesus, Mary, and Joseph begin their long trip from Bethlehem (in front of the fireplace) to Egypt (on top of the television cabinet). The holy family starts its trek, leaving the remaining wise men behind to gaze into an empty manger.

"Once in Egypt, the holy family discovers a penguin and then eats turkey without cranberry sauce," Maria narrates. There is no cranberry sauce in Egypt. That's why the wise men stayed behind. They love cranberry sauce, and there's all they can eat in Bethlehem. Eventually, Thomas the Tank Engine takes the wise men for a ride. Since Jesus is gone, they're going to the circus.

At first, the way Maria and Paul played with their nativity set disturbed me. "They should be more careful with figurines of holy people," I thought. Then I began to realize how lifelike their play really was.

During the weeks before Christmas, I try to focus on the "reason for the season," but often find myself distracted by the pressing concerns of daily life. The fire engine and other unexpected guests that interrupt their tranquil nativity scene aren't all that different from the things in my life that keep me from gazing in awe at the miraculous birth of the infant king. While I struggle to prepare for Christmas, my kids have been prepared since last year. It doesn't occur to them that the Christmas child could ever be separated from their lives.

Once, we lost the nativity set Jesus somewhere in our house. We looked for him high and low. Eventually, we found baby Jesus in Maria's dresser drawer. She had been distraught when she couldn't find him. Once she found Jesus she wouldn't let him go again.

When we leave the house, she'd ask if she could take Jesus with her.

"Yes," I said. "You can take Jesus with you."

"Even when Christmas is over?" she asked.

"Yes," I answered. "Don't leave him behind when Christmas is over. Keep him with you always."

Where's Moses When You Need Him?
Miracles to Rid Your House of Plagues

Noah was good at building arks. Moses was good at getting rid of household pests. When Moses asked for locusts, he got swarms. When he asked that the locusts disappear, they were gone in an instant. Moses was much more effective than the exterminator I paid $189 to rid our house of pests. It's just too bad Moses wasn't invited to my daughter's birthday party a few years ago.

When Maria opened her present and revealed a "Butterfly Garden," I immediately broke into a cold sweat. When I was a boy, I had been given a similar present—a cricket farm that made the sixth plague of Egypt seem like a little bug problem.

A butterfly garden consists of a cardboard terrarium into which you insert live caterpillars and watch them turn into butterflies. The slogan on the box said, "Watch them grow and let them go!" The slogan on my cricket farm must have read, "Watch them grow, watch your cat knock over the terrarium, watch hundreds of crickets scurry into every dark recess of your kitchen."

I learned only three things during my short stint as a cricket farmer. First, the biggest natural predator of crickets is the house cat. Second, a cricket farm accident makes your mom much less receptive to requests for an ant farm. Third, the common garden cricket can live for six months under a Kenmore refrigerator.

Maria's butterfly garden was much more educational. I learned that naming each caterpillar is extremely important. It seems that caterpillar names follow the same convention as ponies and unicorns. Acceptable monikers include "Rainbow," "Princess," and "Beauty." Paul was more enamored with the possibility of hearing the sound caterpillars make when you squash them underfoot. We kept him away from the terrarium until the butterflies were released.

One of the caterpillars died early in the process. I thought it would provide a great opportunity to teach Maria about nature's life cycle. She thought it would be a great time to teach me about funeral planning.

"We have to bury the caterpillar in the yard," she said.

I tried my best to convince her that a certain bathroom fixture provided the glamour of a "burial at sea," but she would hear none of it.

"We'll need a cross to put on the caterpillar's grave too," she said.

Hold on a minute. A cross for an insect's grave? When I was a kid, we wouldn't bury anything smaller than a gerbil, and that was just to keep it from stinking. What's next? A police-escorted funeral procession for the ladybug that succumbed to the front windshield of our car? Who's in charge of this learning experience anyway?!

Obviously, not me.

I made the cross out of two yellow toothpicks. We dug a hole in the mulch and buried the caterpillar in our backyard. No words were spoken. The caterpillar's three-day existence in the butterfly garden spoke for itself. Eat, crawl, eat, crawl. He had lived a full life, even if he hadn't ever gotten his wings.

I didn't take a careful caterpillar census at the beginning of our project, and it's possible that a butterfly escaped in our house. *The Guide to Butterflies* says that each insect can lay 500 eggs at a time. It doesn't mention how long a butterfly can live under a Kenmore refrigerator.

When it comes to indoor plagues, I've faced many life and death situations. I've tracked down and banished birds and bees, mice and squirrels, crabs and spiders. You could say I'm the Crocodile Dundee of indoor, catch-and-release trapping.

One of the most difficult creatures I've had to catch is the bat. My wife and I used to live in an old Victorian house that teemed with vermin. Each June, without fail, bats would serenade us as we slept. I'm usually a pretty sound sleeper, but when a bat is swooping around in my bedroom, diving within inches of my nose, I do the only sensible thing I know: pull the covers over my head until my wife kicks me out of bed to catch the mosquito-breathed varmint.

I have two favorite methods for catching bats. The first is to grab a tennis racket and pretend I'm Pete Sampras and have just been lobbed a shot I can easily smash down the line to win the Wimbledon Championship. Unfortunately, this method is messy and should only be used when you've cornered a bat in an unfinished basement. For furnished areas of the house, I prefer to tape a fishing net onto the end of a broom and play a game of bat lacrosse.

I got used to the drill of catching bats and tossing them out the window with my makeshift lacrosse stick. But I didn't catch them all. One summer morning, my wife was putting on a sneaker when she heard a terrifying screeching sound. Her toes had invaded the home of a sleeping bat.

I tell this story not because I'm worried about your safety but because I relish the thought of thousands of people shaking their shoes upside down every day for the rest of their lives. That's the power of the pen. Remember, the bat was hiding way down deep inside my wife's sneaker—near the toe. You may want to wear sandals for the next ten years until you forget that story. But even bats can't compare to the most treacherous of beasts: the Sparrowdactyl.

My indoor safari began when friends were leaving our house one day. As they opened the front door, in flew a sparrow. But this was no ordinary sparrow. While outside, it was tiny. Once inside the confines of our house, it looked more like a pterodactyl. Or, more accurately, a Sparrowdactyl.

In twenty years, when I recount the story of the Sparrowdactyl to my grandchildren, I will describe the beast's claws which could easily snatch up unsuspecting cows as they peacefully grazed in the field and its beak that could skewer a full-grown pig and swallow it in a single gulp.

I quickly cornered the Sparrowdactyl in our bedroom closet and just as quickly quarantined my kids downstairs before they could get a good look at it. I didn't want them to blow my story for the grandkids. The less they saw, the better.

I entered the closet armed with only a large Rubbermaid storage container and a coat hanger that I used like a lion tamer's whip. I kept the Sparrowdactyl at a safe distance so its razor-sharp beak couldn't do to me what I had seen happen in Alfred Hitchcock's *The Birds*. If only the actors in *The Birds* had enough sense to carry a supply of Rubbermaid containers and coat hangers, they would have been safe. (Perhaps the Sparrowdactyl was miffed that I never finished my birdfeeder in junior high shop class.)

I screamed twice during my hour-long battle in the closet. Both times the prehistoric beast swooped directly above my head, threatening to pelt me with partially digested worms. Eventually, after trying every animal trapping technique I had ever seen on the television program *Wild Kingdom*, I prayed for deliverance.

I carefully positioned my Rubbermaid container and—botta bing, botta boom—I had the bird trapped within seconds. God does good work.

I'm just glad our friends hadn't left by the back door. I've seen deer in our backyard and Rubbermaid doesn't make a "stag-size" container. Besides, I don't like the thought of being alone in my closet for an hour with an animal with antlers.

With butterflies, bats, and Sparrowdacti, the minor miracle is just getting them out of the house. But if you're not careful while eradicating houseflies, your kids may actually teach you something. Humility, for instance.

My wife and I try hard to instill values in our children—to pass on a moral code that will stick with them their entire life. We try to model the seven virtues—prudence, justice, fortitude, temperance, faith, hope, and charity. But instead of teaching the seven virtues, we taught our children the fine art of sarcasm instead. It happened because my wife and I are allergic to dogs and won't get our kids a puppy. (Early childhood experts might argue young children do not understand sarcasm. To such comments, my son replies, "You are so naive.")

I first detected our kids' budding sense of sarcasm when I was about to swat a fly with a rolled-up magazine. The children shrieked in unison, "Don't kill Dave!" They had adopted a fly in lieu of a puppy.

I have known only one other person who had a pet fly. Ray (the person, not the fly) was a sixth-grade classmate of mine. He had the unique ability to catch a fly, pull a hair from his own head, tie a small noose in it, and lasso one of the fly's legs. The tethered fly would buzz around in circles as Ray held its leash. I suspect that Ray's parents were also allergic to dogs.

My only option was to catch Dave alive and release him outside. Unlike Sparrowdactyl hunting, Rubbermaid containers are not helpful for catching flies. You have to face flies eye-to-eye and snatch them out of the air in your bare hand. That's not easy since flies have so many eyes.

On my twenty-seventh attempt, Dave was mine. I could feel him crawling inside my clenched fist. I triumphantly announced that I had caught Dave and was going to set him free.

"That's not Dave," Maria politely informed me. "You caught Mike."

Mike!? (I tossed Mike out the door.)

"Do you have any other pet flies besides Dave and Mike?" I inquired.

"There's Mean Joe," she answered.

Maria didn't tell me why Joe was mean. I can only assume Joe had a traumatic experience with a maggot that forever tainted his personality. Eventually, Mean Joe joined Mike outside. I never did catch Dave.

A few weeks later, I asked Paul if he had seen Dave lately.

"Dave went outside," he said, setting me up.

"Why did he go outside?" I asked.

"He didn't like you," Paul stated, matter-of-factly. Not a bad retort. But, he wasn't finished.

"Dave thought our house was ooooie," he added. "Oooie" is a word Paul uses to describe dirty diapers and pieces of banana that he's dropped like land mines on the kitchen floor.

Our kids had become masters of sarcasm.

Now, most parents don't want sarcastic kids. But, in case your home is a little too quiet and you'd like to spice up the conversation, I can tell you the secret to getting them. The technique is useful for passing on any negative trait to your children and can be accomplished without the aid of common household pests. You lead by example.

The next time you're in a hurry to make a purchase at your local department store and the clerks are too busy talking among themselves to help you, turn to your child and say in a loud voice, "This would be a good place to open a department store." (Don't worry about offending the clerks. I have yet to meet a clerk who understands sarcasm. Besides, your child's education is your highest priority.)

As your child watches you use sarcasm, his or her knowledge will grow. And then one day—botta bing, botta boom—your child's brain cells that control sarcasm will come to life and you'll experience the following scenario.

You'll have to attend yet another late-night meeting, keeping you from eating dinner with the family. You'll gather the kids around the table to explain the importance of tonight's meeting and why you must order pizza for the third straight night. Then, your oldest child will turn to you and say, "This would be a great place to open a kitchen."

What should your reaction be? I highly recommend pretending you are a department store clerk who doesn't understand sarcasm. Either that or take a cue from Moses and head out into the desert for forty years.

Finding First Base—
The Miracle of Sports

Apparently, the apostle Paul never attended a T-ball game. In his second letter to Timothy, Paul wrote, "And in the case of an athlete, no one is crowned without competing according to the rules." I have yet to meet a T-ball player who knows the rules of baseball, yet they all get trophies at the end of the season. Saint Paul must have watched parents at little league games, though, because later on in his letter to Timothy he wrote, "Have nothing to do with stupid and senseless controversies; you know that they breed quarrels." That's good advice for the parents who are hot under the collar because their son was just thrown out at home.

I've experienced miracles at many athletic events. I'm not talking about a last-second pass to win a Super Bowl game or an extra-inning home run to win the World Series. I'm talking about the minor miracles that happen during children's sporting events. Sometimes the miracles are as simple as finding which playing field your child is supposed to be on. Other times it is as miraculous as your son remembering where first base is located.

I wasn't prepared to enjoy watching Paul play T-ball. I suspected the games would be slow and tedious. But when T-ball ended, I missed the unpredictable, fast action that only five-year-old boys can bring. Where else do you see unassisted triple plays in back-to-back innings and players who have the fine-tuned teamwork of a litter of puppies? What other sport's athletes not only play for the love of the game but also for the snack at the end? When I missed a game, Paul beamed as he told me he got two hits but had even more exciting news. "Dad!" he said, licking his lips. "We each got our own pack of Oreos!" If professional baseball owners were smart, they'd sign T-ball players to lifetime contracts. The players would sign on the dotted line for peanuts—especially if they were chocolate covered.

Some people think T-ball is like watching Abbott and Costello's famous "Who's on First?" comedy routine. I disagree. Five-year-olds don't care who's on first. They're asking, "Where is first?"

On my son's team, the coach began by teaching the basics. "You can't get someone out by throwing the ball at them. Don't pick up the dirt. Don't kick the dirt. You can't get someone out by throwing dirt at them." And the most important rule, "After you hit the ball, run to first base."

"Where's first base?" asked Johnny, who looked remarkably like Bud Abbott.

"It's easy to remember where first is, it's always to your right," said the coach.

"Which is my right? I forget," asked Johnny.

"Your right hand is the one you throw the ball with, not the one you wear your glove on," the coach explained.

"But, sometimes I wear my glove on the wrong hand," Johnny sighed.

"See Billy? He's playing first base," explained the coach. "After you hit the ball, run to where Billy is."

Johnny hit the ball and ran to where Billy was. Unfortunately, Billy forgot to use the bathroom before the game and was running toward the Porta-John three fields over—with Johnny right behind him.

T-ball players do get distracted at times. During one game, a player pointed toward center field as he took the plate. At first it appeared he was imitating Babe Ruth, showing the fans where he was going to hit a home run. Then I heard the sound of the ice cream truck passing by. The entire team turned and started walking—as if in a trance—toward the truck. All, except for the second baseman who was writing his name in the dirt, and the first baseman who was trying to catch a butterfly, and the right fielder who was practicing his somersaults.

After the T-ball season ended, I signed my kids up for a bowling league. Bowling isn't as complicated a game as T-ball (no ice cream truck distractions or dirt to play with), and I thought it would be a good way to improve their hand/eye coordination.

When I was about ten, I was on a bowling team that came in second place in a Massachusetts state tournament. I still have the lime green bowling shirt I wore during that tournament. The black felt letters on the back read

"Greenfield Cooperative Bank." It made quite a fashion statement.

When I showed the shirt to my kids, they insisted on wearing it when they bowled. On alternating weeks each wore the green championship shirt. None of the other parents asked me where they could buy a similar shirt for their kids. I guess they were just jealous.

Like T-ball, all the bowlers in the league received trophies. My kids managed to bowl without too many catastrophes, and they enjoyed it. They threw a few balls into the wrong lane and dropped a ball on my foot, but that was about it. Then they became enamored with Tiger Woods, and a family tradition began. It's a weekly tradition, but it's kind of a secret too. The secret is this: There is a miniature golf course in Yellow Springs, Ohio, that is open right through the winter.

Okay, it's not quite a secret, but it's not heavily promoted either. People forget miniature golf as soon as summer is over. But the miniature golf course at Young's Dairy Farm is always open—even when it snows.

Although the course is officially open, the clubhouse door leading out to the barnyard-themed greens is usually locked when we arrive in the winter months. The clerk spends most of his solitary hours waiting for the few driving range customers who enjoy honing their long irons in the heated tee boxes.

"I didn't unlock the door because I didn't think anyone would be playing tonight," says the clerk.

Did I mention we play at night? My wife says when it comes to using good judgment, "my golf bag is a few clubs short."

Winter miniature golf is a game of speed. I tell the clerk we will be back in eight minutes. He's new, so he laughs. We're back in seven minutes, thirty-two seconds—a new course record made possible by a twenty-degree temperature combined with a piercing fifteen-mile-an-hour wind. But what a glorious seven minutes and thirty-two seconds it is!

When the clerk flips the switch for the colored lights that shine on each hole and turns on the music piped in through speakers disguised as plastic boulders, the links come alive. We are alone on the course. The cold wind in our faces makes our eyes water. My ears are so cold they throb. We are in heaven—except for my wife, who stays inside where it's warm.

We tackle the course with reckless abandon. My oldest two children and I hit our balls at the same time, sometimes knocking each other's in on purpose to keep our momentum going.

Annie is content to hold her pink golf ball and dance between each hole. She bounces and hops to Aretha Franklin's "R-E-S-P-E-C-T" between holes ten and eleven and "Jingle Bell Rock" at the fifteenth tee. It costs me a buck to let her dance and run from green to green while carrying a ball and club. It's one of the best bargains in Yellow Springs—even better than ninety-nine-cent burger night at the dairy farm's sandwich shop.

Like my wife and the clerk, you may wonder why we play miniature golf on cold winter nights. Like Tevye from *Fiddler on the Roof*, I will tell you: Tradition.

We have been coming to Young's Dairy Farm to play miniature golf and eat sandwiches every week for the past five years. While I haven't counted the score cards, I can safely say Maria has played more than 200 rounds of golf. I'm confident she will receive a full scholarship to Ohio State University for playing NCAA Division I miniature golf.

Maria will also be selected for the 2016 Olympic miniature golf team, where her years of winter miniature golf training will pay off as she easily wins the gold medal on a dairy farm course in the frigid mountains of Zabljak, Montenegro. (Coincidentally, Yellow Springs will have lost the bid for the 2016 Olympics. Some will claim bribes were involved.)

Until then, playing miniature golf each week, straight through the winter, is a cold, proud tradition that will continue in our family. But please don't tell anyone. The last thing we need is golfers driving in from northern New Jersey, where the miniature golf courses are always mobbed, to get an easy tee time on our course.

While my children have played many sports, none has taught me more than figure skating. The things I've learned make the $10 an hour we pay seem worthwhile. Here are some of the sage bits of wisdom I've gathered while freezing in the stands.

Keep your expectations low. If you have no expectations that your child will ever stand up on the ice for more than five seconds, you will be presently surprised by his or her ninth lesson. Some parents' expectations of success for their kids are just too high. I don't expect that Maria will ever make the Olympic Team . . . but I do secretly hope for it. (You'd think having her play miniature golf in the Olympics would satisfy me.) As I understand it, the Olympic Team pays for all skate rentals, which could save me a bundle. Also, I've heard it is the Olympic coach's responsibility to escort the skaters to the restroom. Those two things would make the many years of sacrifice worth it.

On the off chance Maria does have Olympic ability, I bring my video camera to her lessons now and then. I'm sure NBC will need footage of her for one of their "Olympic Moment" segments. I watched hours and hours of the last Olympics to help me get just the right type of clips.

What impressed me most about the Olympic athletes was how many had to get up two hours before they went to bed so they could milk the cows, feed the sheep, shear the sheep, spin yarn, and knit a sweater to keep them warm on the 600-mile walk to their training facility. (The more productive athletes found the time to discover cures for major illnesses between feeding the cows and shearing the sheep.)

Maria's life is much too easy. We wake up on Saturday mornings, have a leisurely breakfast, and then drive ten minutes to the rink—fifteen minutes if I stop for a cup of coffee. To add some adversity to her life, I've decided to have her squeeze her own orange juice and make her own toast from now on. What a great "Olympic Moment" that will make.

A second bit of wisdom I learned at the rink is to bring correct change. One of the television ads during the last Olympic games told viewers not to forget their VISA card because American Express isn't accepted at the Olympics. The skating rink Maria attends isn't quite as sophisticated, but the vending machines have required exact change in the past. Having the correct change is critical, because Annie is interested in one thing and one thing only when she goes to her sister's skating lessons—eating pretzels. (Although she once watched the Zamboni clean the ice and was impressed by that too.) No pretzels and I've got one whiny kid on my hands. Left unfed, she may decide to look for things to eat under the bleachers. You don't want to have to explain to the emergency room doctor why your daughter ate an entire mitten that had some old M&Ms stuck to it.

Here's some more sound advice: When you fall, don't take others down with you. Professional figure-skating pairs perform a move called the death spiral, in which the man holds his partner's hand as she spins in circles, closer and closer to the ice. The kid's version of the death spiral requires one skater's feet to go out from under him, his arms flailing wildly so that he takes down three or more nearby skaters. If synchronized falling becomes an Olympic sport, I've seen some champions.

I also learned that modesty is the best policy. Maria loves to watch professional figure skating on television. She mimics the skaters' moves across our family room carpet. I'm concerned that she will want to mimic the skaters' outfits too. Several of today's top skaters make the latest MTV star look like she's wearing too many layers. If my daughter makes it to the pros, she'll be wearing a winter coat, gloves, and a hat pulled down over her ears.

There were a few more things I learned watching Maria skate. When you fall, get back up again. Work hard even when the teacher isn't watching. Let others help you up when you're down. And, most important, don't mention how goofy looking that one kid on the ice is—his dad is standing right next to you.

I've also learned a bit from Maria's playtime during school recess. Sometimes I think second graders are the wisest people on the planet. Much of their advanced knowledge comes from learning to make decisions quickly on the playground. When recess is only twenty minutes, you need to pick teams and get on with the game.

One day, Maria was in our driveway with some friends trying to decide what game to play next. That's when I heard the familiar refrain "Bubble gum, bubble gum in a dish, how many pieces do you wish. . . ."

I stopped dead in my tracks. "Bubble gum, bubble gum" is a "picking game" of the "one potato, two potato" variety. It's also the way I made decisions in second grade—thirty-three years ago. I was in awe. Management theories come and go. Negotiation techniques are here today and gone tomorrow. Political philosophies fade away. But "Bubble gum, bubble gum" had stood the rough-and-tumble test of playground time. It was still rock solid.

"Bubble gum, bubble gum" should be made the cornerstone dispute resolution method, especially in the business world. I could be wrong though. "Inky binky bonkey" might be better.

> **Inky binky bonkey**
>
> **Daddy had a donkey**
>
> **Donkey died**
>
> **Daddy cried**
>
> **Inky binky bonkey**

The person whose hand gets the "key" of the last "bonkey" is out. Simply ingenious! If that's not a great way to resolve the next airline management/labor dispute, I don't know what is. Last one in gets to decide what to do with the pension fund.

The amazing thing about "Inky binky bonkey" is that not a word has changed in decades. You would at least have thought it would have been updated for the times. Something like:

> **Inky binky bonkey**
>
> **Daddy has an SUV**
>
> **Guzzled gas**
>
> **No more cash**
>
> **Inky binky bonkey**

If we had only sent in a second-grader instead of the Supreme Court during the Bush-Gore presidential election, the vote counting discrepancies would have been resolved much quicker.

Second-grader: **Mr. Bush, Mr. Gore, please put out one fist each. Engine, engine number nine, coming down Chicago line, if your train goes off the track, do you want your money back? Mr. Gore, your answer?**

Gore: **I've always been in favor of government subsidies for transportation infrastructure. If my plan had been enacted, the track would have been properly maintained and the train wouldn't have derailed.**

Second grader: **A simple "yes" or "no" please, Mr. Gore.**

Gore: **Uhhh . . . no.**

Second-grader: **N-O and you will not be it . . . congratulations, Mr. Bush, you're the president of the United States.**

Gore: **I knew we should have done "Inky binky bonkey."**

If the television networks were smart, they'd make Maria the host of the next *Survivor* reality show. Instead of an exotic location like *Survivor: Amazon*, it could be filmed right here in our town and renamed something that would draw in a younger demographic—*Survivor: Washington Elementary Playground*, for instance. The show would start with twenty kids and be over in ten seconds, allowing enough time for a kickball game before the recess bell rings.

How do you condense a program that usually takes thirty days down to ten seconds? Like this:

> **Inka binka bottle of ink,**
>
> **the cork fell off and you stink,**
>
> **not because you're dirty,**
>
> **not because you're clean,**
>
> **just because ya kissed a boy**
>
> **behind a mag-a-zine.**

"You're the survivor, Jenny," Maria would announce in botta-bing-botta-boom fashion. "Now let's beat the boys at kickball."

Miracles in the Air

The Bible doesn't talk much about flying on airplanes. It mentions some angels flying and even the "flight to Egypt," but nothing about planes. On the flight to Egypt, Joseph, Mary, and baby Jesus traveled on a donkey, which must have been more comfortable than the last seat I had flying in coach. I can relate to the Holy Family's trip because traveling with three young children often makes me feel like a pack mule. Once the car seats, diaper bag, backpacks, snacks, toys, and books are loaded on my back, off I go, hee haw, hee haw. Eventually, my wife is able to prod me along to the plane where I struggle up the aisle, bumping into seats and passengers until I can dump my load. That's when the real adventure begins.

Because of my expertise in flying with children, I was once interviewed for an article by a major Spanish-language Web site. I was confident of my ability to converse in Spanish with the reporter, as long as she kept her questions focused on counting from one to ten and reciting colors and the names of animals. Fortunately for me, she was bilingual.

When the reporter sent me the finished article, I was amazed to see my quotes in Spanish. Then it dawned on me that I can't read Spanish. This would come as no surprise to my college Spanish professor, who told me as much in red ink on every exam. Fortunately for me, I found some free language-translation software. Unfortunately for me, it wasn't the best software.

When I translated my Spanish interview into English, I discovered I had given such profound advice as, "It flies better with your drinks." I've lived my life by that motto, which has been handed down in my family for three generations. It may have first been uttered by my great, great, great grandfather, right before he was killed by the cow.

In the diverse world we live in, you may fly with passengers who don't speak English. Perhaps you're even considering a family trip to Puerto Rico and want to be able to converse in Spanish with the flight attendants. For your convenience, I used the handy language-translation software to provide some of the most common phrases used by parents during plane trips.

Repeat after me.

Estoy apesadumbrado que mi hijo puso sus cacahuetes miel-asados encima de su nariz.

Translation: **I'm sorry that my son put your honey-roasted peanuts up his nose. (This phrase can also mean, "I'm sorry that my son put HIS honey-roasted peanuts up YOUR nose," which is just as likely to occur.)**

No hay lugar para disponer del pañal de mi bebé, así que lo oculté en su bolsillo de la capa.

Translation: There is no place to dispose of my baby's diaper, so I hid it in your coat pocket.

Mi hija no significó quitar su hairpiece. Ella no tenía una servilleta y necesitado algo limpiar la jalea de ella las manos.

Translation: My daughter didn't mean to remove your hairpiece. She didn't have a napkin and needed something to wipe the jelly off her hands.

Sí, ése es mi hijo hacia fuera en el ala. Le dije jugar el exterior mientras que estoy mirando la película.

Translation: Yes, that is my son out on the wing. I told him to play outside while I'm watching the movie.

Puede mi paseo de la hija en el carro de la bebida como usted lo empuja traga el pasillo?

Translation: May my daughter ride on the drink cart as you push it down the aisle?

In case you are traveling through Europe, I translated the phrase, "There is no place to dispose of my baby's diaper, so I hid it in your coat pocket," from English to

German; German to French; and French to English. The final translation read:

"There is no place to disencumber my baby, then dissimulates to him in your ash of coating."

I have never had to disencumber a baby, but I did have to de-cucumber my son once after he inserted a piece of salad in his ear.

If you are not traveling with your own children, you may be subjected to other people's precious ones. Here are some common phrases for you to use.

El olor del pañal de su niño está haciendo mi agua de los ojos.

Translation: **The smell of your child's diaper is making my eyes water.**

Instruya por favor a su niño para obtener su reparte de la sosa. El se funde los cubitos de hielo.

Translation: **Please instruct your child to get his hand out of my soda. He's melting the ice cubes.**

In this case, it flies better without your drink.

Once you've mastered these useful phrases, you're ready for my other flying tips. Keeping your children in their seats can be difficult during a long flight. Naturally, young children would prefer to wander up and down the aisle than sit for three or four hours. That's why it's imperative to tell your children that monsters live under their seats. (Hey, if it works to keep them in their beds at night, it can work on an airplane.)

One mother to whom I suggested this technique said her daughter was only two and didn't know about monsters yet. That's what video rental stores are for. Five or six viewings of *The Mummy* and *Frankenstein* the night before your flight and your kids will know what a monster is.

It's useful to get airline personnel to corroborate your story. This is easily accomplished by telling your children that the kind of monsters that live under the seats are "exits." When the flight attendant is preparing for takeoff and announces that "exits" can be found at the back, middle, and front of the plane, your kids' eyes will bug out of their heads.

Once you've frightened your children into their seats, you'll need to figure out how to entertain them during the flight. Preparing a few travel games for the flight is a great way to help pass the time. Portable video games are fine, but it's nice to play things that get the entire family involved. Passenger bingo is a game everyone can enjoy.

To begin, each member of the family is assigned five seat numbers that can be easily observed. If the person in a seat presses his or her flight attendant call button, the child who has been assigned that seat gets a point. The first person to have all five of his or her seats' call buttons activated is the winner.

For the first few minutes, your children will stay focused watching to see if any buttons are pushed. But, on many flights, passengers don't have enough requests for flight attendants, and the game can get kind of slow. There are a few tricks you can use to get the buttons buzzing for your kids. The first is to walk up the aisle mentioning to passengers that you heard the pilot's daughter is on board because it's take-your-child-to-work day and the pilot plans to let her land the plane. That's usually good for getting a dozen of more passengers to call for a flight attendant. Another way to make the game exciting is to instruct your children to sing "100 Bottles of Soda on the Wall" while the in-flight movie is playing. The song is usually even more effective than the rumor about the pilot's daughter. If the game is really slow, you can shout, "The first ten people who press their attendant call button will receive a free round-trip ticket anywhere in the United States." This should be used only when the flight is almost over and there's still no winner. Passenger bingo isn't only fun to play but—if first class isn't full—you may get bumped up so your family can't bother as many people.

I've often wondered why parents would pay for their kids to sit in first class. After all, why would a sane individual spend thousands of dollars for an infant to sit in a large leather chair and eat fine food, when that same child is content to wear a wet diaper, sit on the ground, and eat gravel?

On one trip, I discovered that you don't actually have to pay for the privilege of annoying first class passengers with your children—the airline may pick up the tab. When our flight was canceled due to snow, the airline rebooked our family and put us in the expensive seats. Since first class is always seated before coach, we got to watch the rest of the passengers board. We also got to listen to their comments. One young girl asked her mom, "Why can't we sit up here?" Her mom told her, with her best snotty attitude, that the seats were only for the rich.

I became self-conscious as more and more passengers stared at me sitting next to Paul. Part of me wanted to explain that we had been lucky enough to get bumped up to first class. Another part of me wanted to play the part of those who routinely pay for and fly first class. I could have improvised a conversation for the coach passengers to overhear as they made their way to the back of the plane.

"The President wants me to serve as Ambassador to France," I might have bragged to Paul. "But Bill Gates still needs my help with Microsoft." It might have worked if I were sitting next to my wife. Talking to a five-year-old wouldn't have been as convincing.

The professional athlete route was another alternative. I could have regaled Paul with stories about my six Olympic gold medals in some obscure equestrian events. The combination of my physique with the fact that a CBS sports broadcaster was sitting across the aisle from me would have blown my cover.

There is a curtain pulled across the doorway between coach and first class. The curtain prevents those in first class from feeling guilty as they eat filet and shrimp and sip the finest wines while their counterparts in coach enjoy small bags of snack mix and four-ounce beverages. (Recipe for airline snack mix: Sweep your kitchen floor. Pour contents on a cookie sheet. Sprinkle with chili powder. Bake until black.)

The curtain also hides the dozens of flight attendants who are at your beck and call. First class is a great training ground for future grandparents. Shortly after we were seated, Paul shouted, "I want apple juice!" Within seconds a flight attendant granted his wish. Paul's eyes were wide. "I have apple juice and we haven't taken off yet, Dad!" he exclaimed. Usually I have to tell Paul thirty to forty times that he will get apple juice *after* we are in the air, and then he will get a single glass. Or should I say plastic cup. Real glasses are reserved for those in first class.

Paul's apple juice came straight up. My Diet Coke was on the rocks. "We're in first class," I said to Paul. "We can drink all we want." By the end of the flight we both floated off the plane.

With his newfound confidence, Paul decided to test what else he could wish for. "I want a snack," he yelled before I could quiet him. Botta bing, botta boom—a flight attendant instantly produced a basket of cookies, crackers, and pretzels. I took a cookie and gave it to Paul. The flight attendant took a handful of snacks and put them on Paul's tray. He was in snack-food heaven.

I don't know where Paul's next question came from, but I clearly heard him ask, "Will the pilot wash our feet?" I suspect that after two successful wishes being granted, he wanted to test just how far his demands would go. I told Paul that there would be no feet washing and that it wasn't even bath night. I'm just glad Paul didn't yell the question because I'm sure the flight attendant would have washed his feet had the pilot refused.

Arriving at our final destination is always a minor miracle for me. After dozens of flights with our children, I know that when God gave us dominion over the birds of the air he wasn't talking about the major airlines. "O that I had wings like a dove! I would fly away and be at rest," says Psalm 55. If I had wings like a dove, not only would I be at rest, but I wouldn't have to worry about lost luggage either.

God's Big Aquarium and the Miracle of Easter

Easter is a time of rebirth. We wear bright clothes to show that winter is over. Flowers begin to bloom. To celebrate, we color eggs—a symbol of new life. And, in our family, we visit Taco Bell, one of the most vivid symbols of new life.

Taco Bell wasn't always a symbol of new life for us. It used to be just another fast food place, albeit the only one where I could order a Beef Baja Chalupa. But then, one *muy loco* day, all of that changed.

It was Mother's Day, and my wife had taken Maria shopping. When lunchtime approached, they decided to stop at Taco Bell for a bite to eat. Maria ordered a chicken soft taco. My wife got a chicken quesadilla, and nine and a half months later a baby. You won't find the baby on the menu. You have to special order it, which is exactly what Maria did.

Amid bites of Mexican processed cheese and salsa, my wife told Maria about a friend of ours who had just had a baby. Maria stopped her in mid-sentence.

"Mommy, I want you to have a new baby," she said. Then Maria closed her eyes, folded her hands, and prayed silently. Nine and a half months later—botta bing, botta boom—Annie was born. She was born just before Easter too.

I know God is everywhere, but who would have thought he hangs out at Taco Bell? He must be there to listen for prayers. I doubt he's there for the Seven Layer Burrito.

Food is an integral part of Easter, and I don't just mean Mexican fast food. There's cabbage too. Easter has two kinds of cabbage—good cabbage and bad cabbage. The good cabbage arrives in the form of golumpki—cabbage stuffed with beef and rice—lovingly made by an aunt of mine.

When I was growing up, golumpki was one of many Easter food traditions, including kielbasa, Chicken à la king, and a bunny cake with a pink jellybean nose and white coconut fur. All of the relatives on my mom's side of the family came to Easter dinner. There were usually forty of us.

What was unusual was that we had all just seen each other the Sunday before, and the Sunday before that, and the Sunday before that. When I was growing up, all forty of us had dinner together every Sunday evening. My grandfather insisted upon it. He wanted his family around him, and we were glad to oblige. My grandfather would cook hamburgers and hotdogs on the grill and show us what was growing in his garden. He'd often impress me by picking a tomato or onion and biting into it just as if he were eating an apple.

But on Easter, we dressed in our finest outfits, which were a perfect match for the olive green and burnt orange kitchens of the day, and went to my grandparents' house to eat golumpki, the good cabbage.

Bad Easter cabbage comes in the form of a recipe for how to color Easter eggs the old fashioned way, using homemade dyes from boiling different plants. My wife found the recipe in an April 1 newspaper, so I can only guess that it was an April Fools joke on readers. The article said, "Experimenting with natural dyes—the makings of which you probably already have in your kitchen—is a great way to get creative. . . . Part of the fun of natural dyes is that they often produce unexpected results."

I'll admit, the smell was unexpected. My wife made natural dyes out of beets, blueberries, cranberries, and red cabbage. She was like one of the Pilgrim women on their first Easter in America. While she slaved over caldrons of boiling fruits and vegetables, I played the role of a Pilgrim man and went in search of the elusive *Cosby Show* rerun on television.

"The eggs are ready to dye," she called from the kitchen.

"It sure does smell like something died," I called back, not quite hearing her correctly.

The article wasn't kidding when it said, "These eggs are for decorative use only. The flavors of the natural-dye ingredients make them undesirable for eating." Actually, they were undesirable for being in the same room with.

The natural dyes made the eggs beautiful shades of red, purple, and blue, but the smell was overpowering. If it were near Halloween, they would have made great ammunition for the neighborhood kids.

Using natural dyes makes a person appreciate the neon, synthetic colors offered by mass-produced egg coloring kits shipped from Taiwan just in time for Easter. Drop a colored pellet into a cup of warm water and vinegar, and you're ready to dunk your eggs in less than two minutes. No chopping, boiling, straining, or nose holding required. The egg coloring kit box even converts into a handy egg-drying stand, which is more than I can say for the head of red cabbage.

We couldn't let Maria and Paul use the natural dyes because, in addition to stinking, they also stain. (That's why all the Pilgrim kids had purple fingers.) So, Maria and Paul jockeyed for position in front of their favorite synthetic egg dye colors. They kept a strict egg count to ensure neither was shortchanged.

The two rushed through the dying process as if they were on an assembly line with a hundred-egg-per-hour quota to meet. Once their works of art were finished and dry, the full egg container went back into the refrigerator where it stayed until Pentecost. Every year, we know it's Pentecost when the eggs are thrown away. If no one has eaten them in forty days, they're not going to be eaten.

Waiting is a big part of the Easter mystery. In addition to waiting for the cabbage smell to dissipate from the kitchen, there's also the waiting and praying that takes place during the Lenten season. While Maria's Taco Bell prayer was answered quickly, sometimes we have to wait a long time before God answers our prayers. God has good reason for delaying his response to our requests. He's busy feeding the goldfish. Sixteen kazillion goldfish, to be exact. At least, that's what my kids tell me.

Swimmy the goldfish should have died long ago. Goldfish have a life expectancy just longer than a fruit fly. Swimmy survived when we went on vacation and pawned him and his blue gravel-filled bowl to a friend. My wife and I fully expected Swimmy would be dead when we returned.

We don't use the word "dead" to describe fish that have expired. We've seen the movie *Finding Nemo*. One of the subplots of the movie is a group of fish that are trying to escape from an aquarium in a dentist's office. The fish theorize "all drains lead to the ocean." So, when one of our pet fish dies, we tell the kids that it is time for him or her to "Find Nemo." We all head to the bathroom and send the goldfish on his or her way, to the sea. I'm very thankful for the movie because without it I'd be burying goldfish next to Maria's deceased caterpillar and our backyard would look like a miniature Arlington National Cemetery with a thousand tiny toothpick crosses.

But Swimmy is the exception to the rule. He must come from hearty goldfish stock because he's beaten the odds. He probably has a seventy-five-year-old carp for a grandfather. We eventually resigned ourselves to the fact that Swimmy would be with us for a long-term stay, so we purchased a fancy five-gallon aquarium to replace his one-gallon bowl. While we were setting up his new digs, Swimmy gazed longingly from his cloudy water-filled bowl at his new, lavish home. Once in his new aquarium, Swimmy became the most animated fish I've ever seen. He'd swim so quickly from one side of the tank to the other and back again that I suspected he had ADD—Aquarium Deficit Disorder.

Swimmy wasn't the first goldfish we owned. Goldie was. My wife won Goldie by tossing a Ping-Pong ball into a bowl at a church festival. Our kids were thrilled. I lamented my poor defensive skills. I should have fouled my wife rather than allow her shot to give Goldie a one-way ticket to our home.

I knew Maria and Paul would quickly become attached to their new pet. It took less than an hour for them to fall in love with Goldie. Unfortunately, Goldie lasted only one day before "Finding Nemo."

Maria and Paul were devastated. They cried. It hurts to see your children suffer, even if over something as small as a goldfish. Being a parent means experiencing a constant conversion through which God tears you down, so he can build you back up even stronger than before. Often, the tearing down comes through watching the pain of your children. It forces you to die to yourself to become closer to your children, and God.

The Gospel of John says, "No one has greater love than this, to lay down one's life for one's friends." Parents lay down their lives minute by minute, hour by hour, day by day. We lay down our lives diaper by diaper, skinned knee by skinned knee, bad dream by bad dream. Parenting, like Easter, is all about dying so others can live. And, like Good Friday's sadness turns into Easter's joy, Maria and Paul found happiness through God.

"I think there's a separate heaven for pets," Maria said one day.

"Really?" I questioned. This was the first time she had sprung her pet heaven thesis on me.

"I just made pet heaven up," she confessed. But it was clear she liked the idea.

"What would pet heaven be like?" I asked.

"Pet heaven is right next to people heaven," Maria explained. "People in heaven can visit pet heaven fives times each day."

"So, pet heaven has visiting hours?" I clarified.

"No, you can go any time you want, just five times in a day," she said. "As soon as I get to the real heaven, I'll visit pet heaven so I can feed Goldie."

"And who might be feeding Goldie until then?" I asked.

Maria thought for a moment. "God's feeding Goldie until I get there," she said.

When I was a kid, I had at least twenty goldfish who "Found Nemo." Those, plus Goldie, make twenty-one fish. Add the other goldfish from around the world that have died during the past 2000 years, and I get a total of sixteen kazillion. That's a lot of fish to feed, which is why God may take awhile to answer your prayers, now and then. He's busy feeding the goldfish.

Since Paul wasn't around when Maria explained the "big aquarium in the sky" concept to me, I took him aside later to get his take on where Goldie was. I explained Maria's thesis, including pet visitation limits and who has the job of feeding the fish.

"That's what I was thinking too," he said. "I just hope I get to heaven before Maria, so I can feed Goldie first."

I Am a Modern Miracle

I have a big inheritance coming. The Bible says, "Blessed are the meek, for they will inherit the earth." I am beyond meek. I am old, boring, and in bad shape. But I blame my boringness on my mom.

One day in my early teens, my mother announced that I would forevermore wear gray socks. Not gray argyles. Not a paisley pattern with a hint of gray. Plain, monotone, gray socks.

Mom gave custody of the color brown to my younger brother. My older brother got basic black. There was no vote, and we were not asked if we had a color preference. One day, my sock drawer simply went blah.

My mother wasn't without her reasons for becoming a strict footwear disciplinarian. My brothers and I wore the same size shoes, and it drove Mom crazy trying to tell our socks apart. Color coding her sons was a necessity if the laundry was to get done.

Like other teenage boys, I dreamed of playing major league baseball. But, unlike other boys, I didn't want to make the big leagues because I loved the game—I simply envied certain parts of the Boston Red Sox uniform. For those who don't think it sounds bad having a wardrobe limited to a single color sock, I ask one thing: Don't judge another until you've walked a mile in his gray socks.

There was a family precedent for placing each of us in our single-color sock prison. For a two-year stint, my grandfather decided it would save time if he wore the same outfit each day. Not the exact same suit of clothes but the same color shirt, tie, pants, and jacket. While he may have shaved minutes off his morning routine by limiting his apparel choices, he busted loose from his self-imposed clothing sentence three years earlier than I was furloughed from my Alcatraz gray foot coverings.

I still get giddy when I see racks of multi-colored socks in a department store but I'm over the traumatic memories of gray socks. Now I'm fixated on sneakers.

I bought my first pair of Reebok sneakers more than twenty years ago and have worn the same brand ever since. When Reeboks first hit the stores in the late '70s, with their understated white leather uppers and trendy embroidered UK flag, they were coolness itself. Wearing them made me cool by association.

But when I made my last sneaker purchase, I was shocked by a name change that brought my coolitude into question. What had been ultra-hip twenty years ago were now labeled "Classic." Classic? I stood dumbfounded in the shoe store aisle. Classic could mean only one thing. I opened my wallet and checked my driver's license. Botta bing, botta boom—I had somehow turned forty.

My drivers license might as well have said that I was "classic," which to me means it's not too early to be investing in a cemetery plot. My gravestone will read: "Tim Bete, loving husband, faithful father. His mother made him wear gray socks, and he owned sneakers which were once considered cool."

Obviously, the new "classic" name-change strategy was the brainstorm of some pimply twenty-two-year-old Reebok product manager who had never even seen an 8-track tape, except for the time he went on a high school field trip to the Smithsonian's Museum of Classic Old Stuff That's No Longer Cool. He's probably the same guy who's responsible for my kids' sneakers, which emit a laser light show of color with every step, like someone strapped tiny neon Christmas trees to their feet.

Somehow, I'll find the bright side and come to grips with owning classic sneakers and not being cool. After all, Mom always told me that every gray sock has a silver lining.

When I realized I was old—not cool—I began to reflect on my life. I get the most reflection time when I'm driving (without the kids). Our minivan is my meditation sanctuary. And when Steppenwolf's "Born to Be Wild" comes on the radio as you're driving a minivan with three car seats and enough Graham crackers to sustain a family of four for a month, it's time for some deep reflection.

Profound questions come to mind. For example, is it possible to "Get your motor running, head out on the highway, lookin' for adventure and whatever comes your way" in a vehicle designed to seat seven and a dozen bags of groceries?

What does OSHA have to say about "smoke and lightning" and "heavy metal thunder"? Certainly these things can't be good for your eyes and ears.

Is it legal to "take the world in a love embrace, fire all of my guns at once and explode into space"? Besides the legality, what would the neighbors think?

Then it hit me like a ton of bricks. "Like a true nature's child, I was born, born to be mild." That's "mild" with an "m." "M" as in "milk toast." "M" as in "mawkish." "M" as in "not wild."

When I was young, I sowed a few wild oats. Now I just eat them to make sure I get enough roughage. I once put a live lobster in a high school toilet as a prank, but no serious injuries occurred—although the plumbers were kind of surprised. And there was the time I rode my bike—ten speed, not Harley—to school without permission but that didn't make me Easy Rider. Some kids liked Superman. I preferred Clark Kent. He was mild-mannered.

As I've grown older, my mildness has mellowed. Now, if I am feeling particularly rambunctious, I may opt for a medium-hot chicken wing instead of the mild. Or perhaps have a second cup of coffee, but that has never caused friends to shout, "Rock on, party dude!"

I'm comfortable being mild. I'm even proud of it. I'd consider becoming an activist for the cause of mildness if I didn't think it would be a little too wild to do so.

Unfortunately, some people never get in touch with their mild side. For example, forty-year-old women who dress like the contestants on American Idol and middle-aged men who insist on reliving their glory days by painting their bodies for football games.

The world could use a few more mild souls. People who don't walk on the grass. People who never exceed their twelve allotted items in the express checkout lane at the grocery store. People who think spending a Saturday night at home watching a movie is pretty exciting stuff.

For those who are still leading wild lives, I offer this advice from the great philosopher Lou Reed. "Hey babe, take a walk on the mild side. I said, hey honey, take a walk on the mild side."

These days, my body regularly tells me I'm getting older. I found a memo on my pillow one morning that made it all too clear. During the night there had been a top-secret reorganization.

Unfortunately, the memo wasn't from my employer. It was from my body.

~~~~~~~~~~~~~~~~~~~~~~~~~~~~

Memorandum

To: **All Tim's body parts**

Fr: **Tim's brain**

Re: **Structural reorganization**

While you've all done a great job during the first forty years of Tim's life, I find it necessary to institute a structural reorganization to more accurately describe the corporation we call Tim. Like many corporations, Tim has become bloated. Many of his divisions are sagging. A few sections have expanded into new territories without prior authorization. Please make note of the following changes and new terminology. While reorganizations are difficult, by working together we can be sure Tim will continue to ignore most of us.

Thanks to Krispy Kreme Donuts and a desk job, the ABS (Amalgamated Belly Structure) division has grown by leaps and bounds. To more accurately describe this growth, ABS will now be called the Fully Actualized Tummy division or FAT, for short. FAT has already expanded into most regions of Tim's body. In fact, it is nearly impossible to find part of Tim's body without FAT.

Another expanding area is the CHIN (Chubby Hinges Insulating the Neck) division which has doubled in size. FAT and CHIN are to be commended for their teamwork on this expansion project.

I'm sorry to say that the MUSCLE (Most Useful Squeezable Clamps for Lifting Everything) division is much smaller today than it was in Tim's youth. This reduction did not occur from a layoff but rather from a laydown—Tim lays down every chance he gets. While hope for MUSCLE growth was high when Tim purchased the Bowflex exercise machine, it is now clear that the George Foreman Grill is the only infomercial product he will ever actually use. We expect that, through attrition, more MUSCLE will be eliminated. We are sorry to see MUSCLE go and wish it the best in its future endeavors.

Likewise, there have been significant losses in the HAIR (Happy It All Isn't Receding) division. It appears that most HAIR has left of its own free will.

Some HAIR has found new locations to reside within the corporate structure—the ears and back to be precise.

Finally, the future of the EYES (Evaporating Youth, Evaporating Sight) division is blurry. EYES are having trouble focusing on their work. Action, in the form of corrective lenses, may be required.

Never let it be said that this reorganization only impacted the lesser members of the body. Even I, Tim's BRAIN (Bit Rusty And Intellectually Numb), have been affected by residing for forty years in such a head. While you have always referred to me as BRAIN, you should now call me FORGETFUL, which stands for . . . ah . . . er . . . well . . . it will come to me later.

After reading such a shocking indictment of my body, I moved into high gear. With three young children, I am concerned about my health. I want to have the stamina to keep up with my kids as they grow.

In the past, I've relied on an exercise regime consisting entirely of skating on thin ice, pushing my luck, and wrestling with non-Aristotelian logic to keep fit. Unfortunately, that hasn't created the washboard-like abs that I'd hoped for. That's why I just bought a new piece of exercise equipment—an elliptical trainer. It's a cross between a stationary bicycle and a stair climber, but not as dangerous as riding your bike down a flight of stairs.

I've tried purchasing exercise equipment in the past but each contraption has turned out to be a boomerang trainer—they flew into my house and then circled back out again into the garage where they sat until I gave them away to some other self-deceived soul who thought that regular exercise sounded like a good idea. At least I'm wiser now. I insist that all exercise equipment I purchase be able to double as a place to stack laundry or hang shirts. I'm smarter than I look.

My father-in-law is an avid runner and in great shape. One day after he had been in an all-day meeting at work, he commented that he didn't know how people could sit in one place for so long without moving.

"It's like anything else worthwhile," I explained to him. "It takes practice and patience to become a couch potato." Beginners should start with an hour at a time and a small bag of chips. It could take a Clint Eastwood film festival or the entire *Pride and Prejudice* miniseries before you've worked your way up to four-hour stints without budging from your recliner. Eventually you'll get used to drinking straight out of the two-liter bottle of Coke and devouring entire cases of Slim Jims at a single sitting.

But if you want to follow my example and get in shape, follow these three steps. (Note: In no way are these tips an attempt to provide professional medical advice. If they were, you would receive an incomprehensible bill for $1,204.)

1. **Begin with stretching. It's important to limber up before jumping into one-handed pushups and marathon running. I use the microwave popcorn rule. When your joints make only one or two popping sounds in a ten-second period, you're done.**

2. Choose an exercise that you enjoy. Do it for twenty minutes or until the ambulance arrives, whichever comes first.

3. Spend time cooling down after your strenuous workout. A cool-down period allows the body to regain its natural level of equilibrium. My last cool-down period lasted four years, which gave me plenty of time to sell my exercise equipment.

Even without fancy equipment, my children give me a pretty good workout. At one point I was considering the purchase of a stair-climber exercise machine. Then I realized that each night my kids make me perform twenty repetitions on the fourteen stairs that go from our first to second floors. Either Paul or Maria will inevitably forget an item without which it will be impossible for him or her to sleep.

Paul: **I need something to sleep.**

Me: **What do you need?**

Paul: **I don't know. Bring me something from downstairs, and I'll tell you if it's what I want.**

After seventeen laps up and down the stairs, Paul has a frying pan, our good china, my power drill, the video camera, a pound of bacon, two kitchen chairs, a dictionary, and my golf clubs in his bed. None of these things will help him sleep, but he insists on keeping all of them. Finally—botta bing, botta boom—Paul gives me a clue.

Paul: **I need a car to sleep.**

Me: **Your red toy car?**

Paul: **No, the green one.**

Me: **Where is it?**

Paul: **I don't have it. I saw it in a catalog.**

Me: **Fine, stay awake until Christmas. I'll put on a pot of coffee for you.**

Paul: **You can't do that, Dad.**

Me: **Why not?**

Paul: **The coffeemaker's still in my bed from last night.**

That's when I tell Paul that he's the one pushing his luck and skating on thin ice.

A Miracle-Filled Future

As you can see, God has blessed me with many miracles. He has blessed me with a loving wife who has miraculous superpowers. He has blessed me with the fertility police (annoying as they are), stop-the-clock-itis (and its cure), and the miracle of watching my children be born. He has blessed me with sleepless nights, diapers to change, potty training, and M&Ms.

God helped me survive my son's potty talk and has given me the ability to substitute for the Tooth Fairy. He has soothed my anxieties and blessed me with a home that is full of love. He has blessed me with 672 rules for the kids as well as an endless supply of things for my son to recycle (whether I want him to or not).

God has blessed me with ears to hear the first words spoken by our children (and torrents of nonstop chatter forever after). He has blessed me with a job that puts food on the table (even if our children won't eat it). He has seen me through the stages of parent development and provided a bounty of chocolate French fries, green ketchup, and squid chips.

God has given me the gift of children who obey (now and then) and the ability to create my own parables. He has blessed me with miraculous ways to save money and lullabies not to sing.

God helped me survive junior high wood shop as well as Christmas Eve toy assembly, birds, butterflies, and bats. He has blessed me with a son who is able to find first base and the joy of winter miniature golf. He has blessed me with a house (even if he hasn't given me the skills to maintain it) and allowed me to gaze upon the wisdom of second graders.

God has given me the grace to make it to the airport on time, change a diaper in a plane's restroom, and safely land. He has blessed me with the miracle of me (even if I'm not in quite the same shape I used to be).

And, to handle all of these miracles, God has blessed me with a sense of humor and the ability to laugh. A sense of humor may be the greatest miracle of all because it is the lens through which God shows us minor miracles. A sense of humor is the hearing aid God provides to help us discern the "botta bing, botta boom" moments in our lives.

The Book of Job says, "He will yet fill your mouth with laughter, and your lips with shouts of joy." That's a good verse to remember when you're in the middle of potty training a child. It's a verse many people in the Bible took to heart. Sarah laughed. Abraham laughed. Daniel laughed. And there must have been laughter at the wedding at Cana. What wedding would be complete without laughter? Since God created us in his own image, I assume he enjoys a good laugh too.

God has also blessed me with the knowledge that my life will continue to be filled with minor miracles. Not that I'm a prophet. If I could predict the future, I'm sure it would be bits of useless trivia. For example, in the year 2020, I can predict the following news stories in the Big Dipper edition of *USA Today.*

Disney releases *100,002 Dalmatians:* **When Pongo and Perdita fall into their master's Clone-a-matic, Cruella DeVil gets more than she bargained for. More than 10,000 extras were hired to man pooper scoopers during filming.**

Mergers in the news: U-Haul, Blockbuster Video, Head Skis, Charles Schwab Corp., and Brown Shoe Company have merged to form U Block Head Charlie Brown, Inc. Financial analysts say that while senior management of the new enterprise seem like nice guys, they aren't expected to ever kiss the little red-haired girl or win a baseball game. In other merger news, Indiana Energy has purchased controlling interests in Goddard Industries, Wheaton River Minerals, and Rust-Oleum Corporation. The four companies will form a new venture called In God Wheat Rust. The group originally was created as a limited partnership until the board of directors realized that God's power was unlimited.

> Television news: In an effort to reach audiences in more time zones, *The Tonight Show* will be replaced by the *Today Show*, which will now be called *Good Morning America*, except on the west coast where it will be called *The Late, Late Show*. *Early Today* will be moved back four hours, replacing *Nightline*. *ABC World News Now* will be shown at its regularly scheduled time, which is not now. *CBS Up To The Minute* will still be up-to-the-minute unless you are on the east coast, in which case the news will be two hours old.

Those kinds of predictions don't have much impact on anyone. But here are three predictions I can guarantee will come true and will have a huge impact on my life. In six years, Maria will be a teenager. In eight years, Paul will reach that milestone. Annie won't be far behind. Just the thought of raising three teenagers is enough to start me praying for a miracle.

We recently bought a new car. We usually keep our cars for eight to ten years before selling them. While buying the car, my wife mentioned it would probably be the vehicle with which Maria learns to drive. That's a scary thought. A sixteen-year-old Maria driving a car with me as the passenger. I can almost imagine us sitting together in the car for her first driving lesson. . . .

> "Let's begin with a prayer," I suggest.
> "Dad! Don't you think I'll be a good driver?" Maria questions.

"Of course. I don't want to pray that you'll be a good driver," I say. "I want to pray that I'll be a good passenger. This isn't like watching you learn to play tee ball or learn to figure skate, where I was sitting in the bleachers. I'm not used to being part of the action."

We put on our seat belts and I ask her to start the car.

"Back out of the driveway and drive down the street until you get to the stop sign," I say.

"Should I stop there?" she asks.

"You're a quick learner," I say. "The last time I was this nervous driving with you was when Mom and I brought you home from the hospital just after you were born. You were so tiny and fragile. All the driving instructions I had as a teenager came back to me in a flash . . . check the sideview and rearview mirrors every four seconds . . . keep at least three car lengths between me and the vehicle in front of me . . . hands at the ten o'clock and two o'clock positions on the steering wheel. . . ."

"Is that your way of telling me to adjust my hands?" she asks.

"No, I'm just telling you a story," I say. . . . "But, now that you mention it. . . ."

"You're not going to launch into one of your homemade parables, are you?" Maria asks.

"I was thinking of telling you the story of the prodigal daughter, who never remembered to fill her dad's car with gas after she had driven it," I say. "But, I'll wait until after you get your driver's license. . . . As I was saying, I was nervous driving home with you from the hospital. I had never been a father before, and I wasn't sure what to do. I hadn't even changed a diaper. I didn't have much experience holding babies. And, I never expected anything could feel as wonderful as being a dad. I was presently surprised by the minor miracles too."

"Minor miracles?" she asks.

"Like when you rode your bike without training wheels for the first time," I say. "And when you discovered that you could play with Paul without fighting. And when you passed the test for your driving permit."

"Dad!" she says, rolling her eyes.

"Don't roll your eyes when you're driving—keep them on the road. So maybe the driving permit wasn't a miracle," I say. "Take the left, at the Krispy Kreme."

"Ummm," we both say together, laughing.

"Annie sure was funny when she was a baby," Maria says.

"You and Paul were pretty funny too," I say. "You probably don't remember the time the two of you adopted a fly, or when you first learned to play miniature golf and could barely hold the club. . . . Do you remember when you started kindergarten and I walked you to the sidewalk in front of the school each day? I always watched as you walked the rest of the way into the building. Do you know what I thought about, watching you walk into school?"

"You wondered if you remembered to put a snack in my backpack?" Maria answers.

"No. I wondered what it would be like when I walked you down the aisle at your wedding," I say. "Watch out for the car merging on the left."

"Dad, I was only five?!" she says.

"I know, I know. But dads think crazy things sometimes. . . . Did I ever tell you how God used you to answer a prayer I said in kindergarten?" I ask.

"No," she says. "Tell me."

So, I tell her about my kindergarten prayer, how I searched my coat pockets in vain each day and how thirty-five years later God used her to put the graham crackers in my pocket (as well as a few other presents).

"Do you really believe God did that?" she asks.

"Take the next right," I say. "I do believe God did that. I believe God works in our lives every day, even in the smallest ways. Even with graham crackers and plastic bags."

"Why would God care about graham crackers?" she asks.

"Great question. God cares about graham crackers because he wants to be involved in our lives, even when he doesn't need to be. Do you remember when you were little and you used to help Mom make a cake by stirring the batter?"

"Yes, I loved to do that," she says.

"Do you think Mom really needed your help, or do you think she could have done it quicker and easier herself?" I ask.

Maria thinks for a moment as she's stopped at a red light.

"I never thought about it. I guess she could have done it better and quicker herself."

"Right. That's the way it is with God," I say. "He could do anything better and quicker without us. But he wants to do things with us."

"Why?" she asks.

"For the same reason Mom let you help mix the batter. She loves you and wanted you to be a part of her life. God doesn't care much about efficiency. If he did, he wouldn't use us to help him with his work. He doesn't spill as much batter as we do either."

"I never thought about it that way," she says.

"Someday you'll be a mother and you'll discover that God created parenthood so we could get a glimpse of what his job is like—even if it is on a much smaller scale.

When you're a parent, you're responsible for others in a way no one else is. You have an unconditional love for your children that is impossible to explain. You're given the gift of others who love you and who forgive you when you're wrong. And, you're blessed with minor miracles every day. Miracles that open your eyes to love, laughter, and God."

"Like the time Paul and I poured cold water on you when you were sleeping on the beach?"

"Well, that opened my eyes all right," I say. "And it was pretty funny."

For miles and miles we drive and talk about when she was a little girl, her friends, and hobbies. Through side streets and highways, we talk about school and college and what she wants to do with her life. We chat about important things and unimportant ones.

Then, as I look into the rearview mirror, it's as if I can see God sitting in the back seat. He's the driving instructor's driving instructor. He never takes the wheel from us, but he's always there to encourage us and give us guidance. I imagine God giving me a thumbs up sign and a big grin. And I can tell that there are a lot more minor miracles in store for me.

As we arrive home, Maria pulls the car into our garage. I sit for a moment, deep in thought.

"What's wrong, Dad?" Maria asks. "Are you surprised we made it home alive? Did I make too many mistakes? Did I forget to use my turn signal?"

I pause for a few seconds before answering.

"No," I say. "Your driving was excellent. . . . It just dawned on me that for the past hour, I've had a wonderfully coherent and intelligent conversation with a sixteen-year-old."

You could hear the "botta bing, botta boom" for miles.

BEFORE KIDS

Tim Bete is well known for his award-winning parenting humor column that has been featured in the *Christian Science Monitor* and more than a dozen parenting magazines. His column is the foundation for this book. Tim has also contributed to several books including *Amazing Grace for the Catholic Heart, From the Heart: Stories of Love and Friendship, Misadventures of Moms and Disasters of Dads,* and *Become a Published Writer.*

Formerly the editor of *Early Childhood News* magazine, Tim is presently director of the Erma Bombeck Writers' Workshop at the University of Dayton. He has a bachelor's degree from The Catholic University of America, where he served as one of the university's first resident minister interns. He has since worked in numerous church ministries.

Tim and his wife live in Beavercreek, Ohio, with their three children. His hobbies include pushing his luck, skating on thin ice, and fishing his kids' toys out of the toilet.

AFTER KIDS